TAX Guide for SMALL BUSINESS

Tax Guide for Small Business

How to IRS Proof Your Business

Charlotte Allen, E.A.

Copyright © 2019 by Charlotte Allen, EA

All rights reserved.

ISBN-13:

Table of Contents

SELECTING YOUR BUSINESS ENTITY 1
CASH VS. ACCRUAL ACCOUNTING METHODS 7
EMPLOYEES VS. INDEPENDENT CONTRACTORS 17
KEEPING GOOD RECORDS 20
WHAT IS INCOME? 32
BUSINESS DEDUCTIONS... 39
GROSS PROFIT AND NET PROFIT 80
FILING AND PAYING TAXES 85
YOUR RIGHTS AS A TAXPAYER 91
COMMON TAX MISTAKES to AVOID.. 97
HOW TO GET MORE INFORMATION 99

Chapter 1

SELECTING YOUR BUSINESS ENTITY

There are a few options you have when choosing your business entity. They are:

    Sole Proprietor
    Partnership
    Corporation
    S Corporation
    Limited Liability Company

This is a very important step that will determine your tax reporting requirements. Your business entity will affect how much you pay in taxes, your ability to raise money, the paperwork you need to file, and your personal liability. One question you need to answer is whether you will be the sole owner of the business or whether you will have one or more people who own a percentage of your business.

If you want to retain controlling interest you will need to keep, at least, fifty one percent of the business in your name. You must retain a 100% of the company to be a sole proprietorship.

A partnership must have two or more partners. Partnerships are more complex and require you to file a partnership return form 1065. This is a flow through company so you and the other partners would be taxed on a personal level.

If you elect your business to be a corporation, you will file an 1120 return which is more complicated. You can then have other shareholders who can contribute to your company. You and your shareholders would have no personal liability. This is one of the biggest benefits of a corporation.

You can elect to be a S corporation. With a S corporation you can have from one to one hundred shareholders, but they must all be U.S. citizens. This is a flow through company so you and your shareholders would be taxed on a personal level. You must file an 1120S tax return.

You can, also, select a limited liability company (LLC) status

Determining Which Type of Business to Use

The most common forms of business are the sole proprietorship, partnership, and corporation. When beginning a business, you must decide which form of business to use before you register your business with the state. Legal and tax considerations are part of this decision. Only tax considerations are discussed in this book.

Sole Proprietorships

A sole proprietorship is an unincorporated business that is owned by one individual. It is the simplest form of business organization to start and maintain. The business has no existence apart from you, the owner. Its liabilities are your personal liabilities. You undertake the risks of the business for all assets owned in the business. You include the income and expenses of the business on your personal tax return.

Partnerships

A partnership is the relationship existing between two or more persons who join to carry on a trade or business. Each person contributes money, property, labor, or skill, and expects to share in the profits and losses of the business.

A partnership must file an annual information return (1065) to report the income, deductions, gains, losses, etc., from its operations, but it does not pay income tax. Instead, it "passes through" any profits or losses to its partners. Each partner includes his or her share of the partnership's items on his or her tax return.

Business Owned and Operated by Spouses

If you and your spouse jointly own and operate an unincorporated business and share in the profits and losses, you are partners in a partnership, even if you have no formal partnership agreement. Do not use Schedule C or C-EZ. Instead, file Form 1065, U.S. Return of Partnership Income.

Exception—Community Income

If you and your spouse wholly own an unincorporated business as community property under the community property laws of a state, foreign country, or U.S. possession, you can treat the business either as a sole proprietorship or a partnership. The only states with community property laws are Arizona, California, Idaho, Louisiana, Nevada, New Mexico, Texas, Washington, and Wisconsin.

Exception—Qualified Joint Venture

If you and your spouse each materially participate as the only members of a jointly owned and operated business, and you file a joint return for the tax year, you can make a joint election to be treated as a qualified joint venture instead of a partnership for the tax year. Making this election will allow you to avoid the complexity of Form 1065 but still give each spouse credit for social security earnings on which retirement benefits are based. For an explanation of "material participation," see the Instructions for Schedule C, line G.

To make this election, you must divide all items of income, gain, loss, deduction, and credit attributable to the business between you and your spouse in accordance with your respective interests in the venture. Each of you must file a separate Schedule C or C-EZ and a separate Schedule SE.

Corporations

In forming a corporation, prospective shareholders exchange money, property, or both, for the corporation's capital stock. A corporation generally takes the same deductions as a sole proprietorship to figure its taxable income. A corporation can also take special deductions.

C Corporations

The profit of a C corporation is taxed to the corporation when earned, and then is taxed to the shareholders when distributed as dividends. However, shareholders cannot deduct any loss of the corporation.

S Corporations

An eligible domestic corporation (or a domestic entity eligible to elect to be treated as a corporation) can avoid double taxation (once to the corporation and again to the shareholders) if it meets certain tests and elects to be treated as an S corporation. Generally, an S corporation is exempt from federal income tax other than tax on certain capital gains and passive income. On their tax returns, the S corporation's shareholders include their share of the corporation's separately stated items of income, deduction, loss, and credit, and their share of unseparated stated income or loss. For more information on S corporations and the tests that need to be met to be eligible to elect to be an S corporation, see the instructions for Form 2553, Election by a Small Business Corporation, and Form 1120S, U.S. Income Tax Return for an S Corporation.

Limited Liability Company

A limited liability company (LLC) is an entity formed under state law by filing articles of organization as an LLC. The members of an LLC are not personally liable for its debts. An LLC may be classified for federal income tax purposes as either a partnership, a corporation, or an entity disregarded as separate from its owner by applying the rules in Regulations section 301.7701-3.

More Information

For more information on LLCs, see the instructions for Form 8832, Entity Classification Election. Sole proprietorship is the easiest form of business to start if there is just one owner. If you are considering another type of business, you may want to consult a lawyer to help you create the legal structure of your business. In an IRS audit you may be asked for the legal documents that formed your business and if you apply for loans the lender will want to see these legal documents. A lawyer will advise you of the documents needed for the form of business you decide on and can prepare them for you.
Further information is beyond the scope of this book.
  Be careful in doing this part on your own as it will affect the areas mentioned earlier in this chapter. Remember starting with a sole proprietorship is the easiest form of business to start and you will have less forms to file at tax season. This does not necessarily mean this is the best form of business for your situation.

Chapter 2

CASH VS. ACCRUAL ACCOUNTING METHODS

You must figure your taxable income and file an income tax return for an annual accounting period called a tax year. Also, you must consistently use an accounting method that clearly shows your income and expenses for the tax year.

Accounting Periods

When preparing a statement of income and expenses (generally your income tax return), you must use your books and records for a specific interval of time called an accounting period. The annual accounting period for your income tax return is called a tax year. You can use one of the following tax years.

- A calendar tax year.
- A fiscal tax year.

Unless you have a required tax year, you adopt a tax year by filing your first income tax return using that tax year. A required tax year is a tax year required under the Internal Revenue Code or the Income Tax Regulations.

Calendar Tax Year.

A calendar tax year is 12 consecutive months beginning January 1 and ending December 31. You must adopt the calendar tax year if any of the following apply.
- You do not keep books.
- You have no annual accounting period.
- Your present tax year does not qualify as a fiscal year.
- Your use of the calendar tax year is required under the Internal Revenue Code or the Income Tax Regulations.

If you filed your first income tax return using the calendar tax year and you later begin business as a sole proprietor, you must continue to use the calendar tax year unless you get IRS approval to change it or are otherwise allowed to change it without IRS approval.

If you adopt the calendar tax year, you must maintain your books and records and report your income and expenses for the period from January 1 through December 31 of each year.

Fiscal Tax Year

A fiscal tax year is 12 consecutive months ending on the last day of any month except December. A 52-53-week tax year is a fiscal tax year that varies from 52 to 53 weeks but does not have to end on the last day of a month. If you adopt a fiscal tax year, you must maintain your books and records and report your income and expenses using the same tax year.

Change in Tax Year

Once you adopt an accounting period and file your first return, you must file Form 1128 to change your accounting period. Changing an accounting period once you have adopted a different accounting period is beyond the scope of this book. For further information see chapter 12 on how to get more information regarding any tax questions.

Accounting Methods

An accounting method is a set of rules used to determine when and how income and expenses are reported. Your accounting method includes not only the overall method of accounting you use, but also the accounting treatment you use for any material item. You choose an accounting method for your business when you file your first income tax return that includes a Schedule C, 1065 1120 or 1120S for the business. After that, if you want to change your accounting method, you generally must get IRS approval. See Change in Accounting Method, later.

Kinds of Methods

Generally, you can use any of the following accounting methods.
Cash method.
Accrual method.
Special methods of accounting for certain items of income and expenses.
Combination method using elements of two or more of the above.
You must use the same accounting method to figure your taxable income and to keep your books. Also, you must use an accounting method that clearly shows your income. You can account for business and personal items under different accounting methods. For example, you can figure your business income under an accrual method, even if you use the cash method to figure personal items. If you have two or more separate and distinct businesses, you can use a different accounting method for each if the method clearly reflects the

income of each business. They are separate and distinct only if you maintain complete and separate books and records for each business.

Cash Method

Most individuals and many sole proprietors with no inventory use the cash method because they find it easier to keep cash method records. However, if an inventory is necessary to account for your income, you generally must use an accrual method of accounting for sales and purchases, unless you are a small business taxpayer. Under the cash method, include in your gross income all items of income you actually or constructively receive during your tax year. If you receive property or services, you must include their fair market value in income. Example. On December 30, 2019, Mrs. Sycamore sent you a check for interior decorating services you provided to her. You received the check on January 2, 2020. You must include the amount of the check in income for 2019. You have constructive receipt of income when an amount is credited to your account or made available to you without restriction. You do not need to have possession of it. If you authorize someone to be your agent and receive income for you, you are treated as having received it when your agent received it.

Checks

You cannot hold checks or postpone taking possession of similar property from one tax year to another to avoid paying tax on the income. You must report the income in the year the property is received or made available to you without restriction. Receipt of a valid check by the end of the tax year is constructive receipt of income in that year, even if you cannot cash or deposit the check until the following year.

Debts Paid by Another Person or Canceled

If your debts are paid by another person or are canceled by your creditors, you may have to report part or all of this debt relief as income. If you receive income in this way, you constructively receive the income when the debt is canceled or paid.

Repayment of Income

If you include an amount in income and in a later year you must repay all or part of it, you can usually deduct the repayment in the year in which you make it. If the amount you repay is over $3,000, a special rule applies.

Expenses Under the Cash Method

You generally deduct expenses in the tax year in which you pay them. This includes business expenses for which you contest liability. However, you may not be able to deduct an expense paid in advance or you may be required to capitalize certain costs, as explained later under Uniform Capitalization Rules.

Expenses Paid in Advance

You can deduct an expense you pay in advance only in the year to which it applies. If you pay three years of rent in advance, for example, you can only deduct the rent for the first year and you would deduct the other two years in the subsequent years.

Accrual Method

Under an accrual method of accounting, you generally report income in the year earned and deduct or capitalize expenses in the year incurred. The purpose of an accrual method of accounting is to match income and expenses in the correct year.

Income Under the Accrual Method

You generally include an amount in your gross income for the tax year in which all events that fix your right to receive the income have occurred and you can determine the amount with reasonable accuracy. For a taxpayer with an applicable financial statement or other financial statement as the Secretary may specify, the all-events test for an item of gross income is considered met no later than when included in an applicable financial statement or such other financial statement. Example. You are a calendar year accrual method taxpayer. You sold a computer on December 28, 2018. You billed the customer in the first week of January 2019, but you did not receive payment until February 2019. You must include the amount received for the computer in your 2018 income.

Income—Special Rules

The following are special rules that apply to advance payments, estimating income, and changing a payment schedule for services.

Estimated income

If you include a reasonably estimated amount in gross income, and later determine the exact amount is different, take the difference into account in the tax year in which you make the determination.

Change in Payment Schedule for Services

If you perform services for a basic rate specified in a contract, you must accrue the income at the basic rate, even if you agree to receive payments at a lower rate until you complete the services and then receive the difference.

Advance Payments

Generally, you report an advance payment as income in the year you receive the payment. However, if you receive an advance payment, you can elect to postpone including the advance payment in income until the next tax year. You cannot postpone including any payment beyond that tax year.

Expenses

Under an accrual method of accounting, you generally deduct or capitalize a business expense when both the following apply.

1. **The all-events test has been met.** The test has been met when: a. All events have occurred that fix the fact of liability, and b. The liability can be determined with reasonable accuracy.

2. **Economic performance has occurred.** You generally cannot deduct or capitalize a business expense until economic performance occurs. If your expense is for property or services provided to you, or for your use of property, economic performance occurs as the property or services are provided or as the property is used. If your expense is for property or services you provide to others, economic performance occurs as you provide the property or services.

An exception allows certain recurring items to be treated as incurred during a tax year even though economic performance has not occurred. **Example**. You are a calendar year taxpayer and use an accrual method of accounting. You buy office supplies in December 2018. You receive the supplies and the bill in December, but you pay the bill in January 2019. You can deduct the expense in 2018 because all events that fix the fact of liability have occurred, the amount of the liability could be reasonably determined, and economic performance occurred in that year. Your office supplies may qualify as a recurring expense. In that case, you can deduct them in 2018 even if the supplies are not delivered until 2019 (when economic performance occurs).

Keeping Inventories

When the production, purchase, or sale of merchandise is an income producing factor in your business, you generally must take inventories into account at the beginning and the end of your tax year, unless you are a small business taxpayer. If you must account for an inventory, you generally must use an accrual method of accounting for your purchases and sales.

Special Rule for Related Persons

You cannot deduct business expenses and interest owed to a related person who uses the cash method of accounting until you make the payment and the corresponding amount is includible in the related person's gross income. Determine the relationship, for this rule, as of the end of the tax year for which the expense or interest would otherwise be deductible. If a deduction is not allowed under this rule, the rule will continue to apply even if your relationship with the person ends before the expense or interest is includible in the gross income of that person. Related persons include members of your immediate family, including brothers and sisters (either whole or half), your spouse, ancestors, and lineal descendants. For a list of other related persons, see section 267 of the Internal Revenue Code.

Combination Method

You generally can use any combination of cash, accrual, and special methods of accounting if the combination clearly shows your income and expenses and you use it consistently. However, the following restrictions apply.

If an inventory is necessary to account for your income, you generally must use an accrual method for purchases and sales. You can use the cash method for all other items of income and expenses. If you use the cash method for figuring your income, you must use the cash method for reporting your expenses.

If you use an accrual method for reporting your expenses, you must use an accrual method for figuring your income.

• If you use a combination method that includes the cash method, treat that combination method as the cash method.

Generally, if you produce, purchase, or sell merchandise in your business, you must keep an inventory and use an accrual method for purchases and sales of merchandise. Exception for small business taxpayers. **If you are a small business taxpayer, you can choose not to keep an inventory, but you must still use a method of accounting for inventory that clearly reflects income.** If you choose not to keep an inventory, you won't be treated as failing to clearly reflect income if your method of accounting for inventory treats inventory as non-incidental material or supplies or conforms to your financial accounting treatment of inventories.

If, however, you choose to keep an inventory, you generally must use an accrual method of accounting and value the inventory each year to determine your cost of goods sold in Part III of Schedule C. Small business taxpayer.

Definition of a Small Business

You qualify as a small business taxpayer if you (a) have average annual gross receipts of $25 million or less for the 3 prior tax years, and (b) are not a tax shelter. If your business has not been in existence for all of the 3-tax-year period used in figuring average gross receipts, base your average on the period it has existed, and if your business has a predecessor entity, include the gross receipts of the predecessor entity from the 3-tax-year period when figuring average gross receipts. If your business (or predecessor entity) had short tax years for any of the 3-tax-year period, annualize your business' gross receipts for the short tax years that are part of the 3-tax-year period.

Treating Inventory as Non-incidental Material or Supplies

If you account for inventories as materials and supplies that are not incidental, you deduct the amounts paid to acquire or produce the inventoriable items treated as materials and supplies in the year in which they are first used or consumed in your operations.

Financial Accounting Treatment of Inventories

Your financial accounting treatment of inventories is determined with regard to the method of accounting you use in your applicable financial statement or, if you do not have an applicable financial statement, with regard to the method of accounting you use in your books and records that have been prepared in accordance with your accounting procedures.

Changing Your Method of Accounting for Inventory

If you want to change your method of accounting for inventory, you must file Form 3115.

Items Included in Inventory

If you are required to account for inventories, include the following items when accounting for your inventory.

- Merchandise or stock in trade.
- Raw materials.
- Work in process.
- Finished products.
- Supplies that physically become a part of the item

Chapter Three

EMPLOYEES VS. INDEPENDENT CONTRACTORS

Determining Whether the Individuals Providing Services are Employees or Independent Contractors

Before you can determine how to treat payments you make for services, you must first know the business relationship that exists between you and the person performing the services. The person performing the services may be:

An independent contractor
An employee (common-law employee)
A statutory employee
A statutory nonemployee
A government worker

In determining whether the person providing service is an employee or an independent contractor, all information that provides evidence of the degree of control and independence must be considered.

Common Law Rules

Facts that provide evidence of the degree of control and independence fall into three categories:

Behavioral: Does the company control or have the right to control what the worker does and how the worker does his or her job?

Financial: Are the business aspects of the worker's job controlled by the payer? (these include things like how worker is paid, whether expenses are reimbursed, who provides tools/supplies, etc.)

Type of Relationship: Are there written contracts or employee type benefits (i.e. pension plan, insurance, vacation pay, etc.)? Will the relationship continue and is the work performed a key aspect of the business?

Businesses must weigh all these factors when determining whether a worker is an employee or independent contractor. Some factors may indicate that the worker is an employee, while other factors indicate that the worker is an independent contractor. There is no "magic" or set number of factors that "makes" the worker an employee or an independent contractor, and no one factor stands alone in making this determination. Also, factors which are relevant in one situation may not be relevant in another.

The keys are to look at the entire relationship, consider the degree or extent of the right to direct and control, and finally, to document each of the factors used in coming up with the determination.

Form SS-8

If, after reviewing the three categories of evidence, it is still unclear whether a worker is an employee or an independent contractor, Form SS-8, Determination of Worker Status for Purposes of Federal Employment Taxes and Income Tax Withholding can be filed with the IRS. The form may be filed by either the business or the worker. The IRS will review the facts and circumstances and officially determine the worker's status.

Be aware that it can take at least six months to get a determination, but a business that continually hires the same types of workers to perform particular services may want to consider filing Form SS-8 .

Employment Tax Obligations

Once a determination is made (whether by the business or by the IRS), the next step is filing the appropriate forms and paying the associated taxes.
Forms and associated taxes for independent contractors
Forms and associated taxes for employees
Employment Tax Guidelines
There are specific employment tax guidelines that must be followed for certain industries.
Employment Tax Guidelines: Classifying Certain Van Operators in the Moving

CHAPTER FOUR

KEEPING GOOD RECORDS

Everyone in business must keep records. Good records will help you do the following.

Monitor the Progress of Your Business

You need good records to monitor the progress of your business. Records can show whether your business is improving, which items are selling, or what changes you need to make. Good records can increase the likelihood of business success.

Prepare Your Financial Statements

You need good records to prepare accurate financial statements. These include income (profit and loss) statements and balance sheets. These statements can help you in dealing with your bank or creditors and help you manage your business.

An income statement shows the income and expenses of the business for a given period. A balance sheet shows the assets, liabilities, and your equity in the business on a given date.

Identify Source of Receipts

You will receive money or property from many sources. Your records can identify the source of your receipts. You need this information to separate business from nonbusiness receipts and taxable from nontaxable income.

Keep Track of Deductible Expenses

You may forget expenses when you prepare your tax return unless you record them when they occur.

Prepare Your Tax Returns

You need good records to prepare your tax returns. These records must support the income, expenses, and credits you report. Generally, these are the same records you use to monitor your business and prepare your financial statements.

Support Items Reported on Tax Returns

You must keep your business records available for inspection by the IRS and other taxing authorities. If any of your tax returns are examined, you may be asked to explain the items reported. A complete set of records will speed up the examination.

Kinds of Records to Keep

Except in a few cases, the law does not require any specific kind of records. You can choose any recordkeeping system suited to your business that clearly shows your income and expenses.

The business you are in affects the type of records you need to keep for federal tax purposes. You should set up your recordkeeping system using an accounting method that clearly shows your income for your business. If you are in more than one business, you should keep a complete and separate set of records for each business. A corporation should keep minutes of board of directors' meetings.

Your recordkeeping system should include a summary of your business transactions. This summary is ordinarily made in your books (for example, accounting journals and ledgers). Your books must show your gross income, as well as your deductions and credits. For most small businesses, the business checkbook is the main source for entries in the business books. In addition, you must keep supporting documents.

Electronic Records

All requirements that apply to hard copy books and records also apply to electronic storage systems that maintain tax books and records. When you replace hard copy books and records, you must maintain the electronic storage systems for as long as they are material to the administration of tax law. An electronic storage system is any system for preparing or keeping your records either by electronic imaging or by transfer to an electronic storage media. The electronic storage system must index, store, preserve, retrieve, and reproduce the electronically stored books and records in legible format. All electronic storage systems must provide a complete and accurate record of your data that is accessible to the IRS and other taxing authorities. Electronic storage systems are also subject to the same controls and retention guidelines as those imposed on your original hard copy books and records.

The original hard copy books and records may be destroyed provided that the electronic storage system has been tested to establish that the hard copy books and records are being reproduced in compliance with IRS requirements for an electronic storage system and procedures are established to ensure continued compliance with all applicable rules and regulations. You still have the responsibility of retaining any other books and records that are required to be retained.

The IRS may test your electronic storage system, including the equipment used, indexing methodology, software and retrieval capabilities. This test is not considered an examination and the results must be shared with you. If your electronic storage system meets the requirements mentioned earlier, you will be incompliance. If not, you may be subject to penalties for noncompliance, unless you continue to maintain your original hard copy books and records in a manner that allows you and the IRS to determine your correct tax.

For details on electronic storage system requirements, see Revenue Procedure 97-22, available at www.irs.gov/Tax-Exempt-Bonds/RevenueProcedures.

Supporting Documents

Purchases, sales, payroll, and other transactions you have in your business generate supporting documents. Supporting documents include sales slips, paid bills, invoices, receipts, deposit slips, and canceled checks. These documents contain information you need to record in your books.

It is important to keep these documents because they support the entries in your books and on your tax return. Keep them in an orderly fashion and in a safe place. For instance, organize them by year and type of income or expense.

Gross Receipts

Gross receipts are the income you receive from your business. You should keep supporting documents that show the amounts and sources of your gross receipts. Documents that show gross receipts include the following.
- Cash register tapes.
- Bank deposit slips.
- Receipt books.
- Invoices.
- Credit card charge slips.
- Forms 1099-MISC.

Inventory

Inventory is any item you buy and resell to customers. If you are a manufacturer or producer, this includes the cost of all raw materials or parts purchased for manufacture into finished products. Your supporting documents should show the amount paid and that the amount was for inventory. Documents reporting the cost of inventory include the following.

Canceled checks.
Cash register tape receipts.
Credit card sales slips.
Invoices.

These records will help you determine the value of your inventory at the end of the year. See Publication 538 for information on methods for valuing inventory.

Expenses

Expenses are the costs you incur (other than the cost of inventory) to carry on your business. Your supporting documents should show the amount paid and that the amount was for a business expense. Documents for expenses include the following.

Canceled checks.
Cash register tapes.
Account statements.
Credit card sales slips.
Invoices.
Petty cash slips for small cash payments.

A petty cash fund allows you to make small payments without having to write checks for small amounts. Each time you make a payment from this fund, you should make out a petty cash slip and attach it to your receipt as proof of payment.

Travel, Transportation, Entertainment, and Gift Expenses

Specific recordkeeping rules apply to these expenses including keeping a journal or log of the what, when, where, who and why of expenses related to these items.

Employment Taxes

There are specific employment tax records you must keep. See chapter 8.

Assets

Assets are the property, such as machinery and furniture you own and use in your business. You must keep records to verify certain information about your business assets. You need records to figure the annual depreciation and the gain or loss when you sell the assets. Your records should show the following information.

When and how you acquired the asset.
Purchase price.
Cost of any improvements.
Section 179 deduction taken.
Deductions taken for depreciation.
Deductions taken for casualty losses, such as losses resulting from fires or storms.
How you used the asset.
When and how you disposed of the asset.
Selling price.

Expenses of Sale.
The following documents may show this information.
Purchase and sales invoices.
Real estate closing statements.
Canceled checks.

What If I Don't Have a Canceled Check?

If you do not have a canceled check, you may be able to prove payment with certain financial account statements prepared by financial institutions. These include account statements prepared for the financial institution by a third party. These account statements must be highly legible. The following table lists acceptable account statements.

Proof of payment of an amount, by itself, does not establish you are entitled to a tax deduction. You should also keep other documents, such as credit card sales slips and invoices, to show that you also incurred the cost.

If payment is by:	Then the statement must show:
Check	Check number
	Amount paid
	Payee's name
	Date check posted to your bank account
Electronic Funds Transfer	Amount transferred
	Payee's name
	Date transfer was posted
Credit Card	Amount charged
	Payee's name
	Transaction amount

Recording Business Transactions

A good recordkeeping system includes a summary of your business transactions. (Your business transactions are shown on the supporting documents just discussed.) Business transactions are ordinarily summarized in books called journals and ledgers. You can buy them at your local stationery or office supply store.

A journal is a book where you record each business transaction shown on your supporting documents. You may have to keep separate journals for transactions that occur frequently.

A ledger is a book that contains the totals from all of your journals. It is organized into different accounts.

Whether you keep journals and ledgers and how you keep them depends on the type of business you are in. For example, a recordkeeping system for a small business might include the following items.

Business checkbook.

Daily summary of cash receipts.

Monthly summary of cash receipts.

Check disbursements journal.

Depreciation worksheet.

Employee compensation record. The system you use to record business transactions will be more effective if you follow good recordkeeping practices. For example, record expenses when they occur, and identify the source of recorded receipts.

Business Checkbook

One of the first things you should do when you start a business is open a business checking account. You should keep your business account separate from your personal checking account.

The business checkbook is your basic source of information for recording your business expenses. You should deposit all daily receipts in your business checking account. You should check your account for any errors.

Consider using a checkbook that allows enough space to identify the source of deposits as business income, personal funds, or loans. You should also note on the deposit slip the source of the deposit and keep copies of all slips.

You should make all payments by check to document business expenses. Write checks payable to yourself only when making withdrawals from your business for personal use. Avoid writing checks payable to cash. If you must write a check for cash to pay a business expense, include the receipt for the cash payment in your records. If you cannot get a receipt for a cash payment, you should make an adequate explanation in your records at the time of payment.

Use the business account for business purposes only. Indicate the source of deposits and the type of expense in the checkbook.

Reconciling the Checking Account

When you receive your bank statement, make sure the statement, your checkbook, and your books agree. The statement balance may not agree with the balance in your checkbook and books if the statement:

Includes bank charges you did not enter in your books and subtract from your checkbook balance, or

Does not include deposits made after the statement date or checks that did not clear your account before the statement date.

By reconciling your checking account, you will:
Verify how much money you have in the account,
Verify your checkbook and books reflect all bank charges and the correct balance.
Correct any errors in your bank statement, checkbook, and books.

Employment Taxes

If you have employees, you must keep all employment tax records for at least 4 years after the date the tax becomes due or is paid, whichever is later.

Assets

Keep records relating to property until the period of limitations expires for the year in which you dispose of the property in a taxable disposition. You must keep these records to figure any depreciation, amortization, or depletion deduction, and to figure your basis for computing gain or loss when you sell or otherwise dispose of the property. Generally, if you received property in a nontaxable exchange, your basis in that property is the same as the basis of the property you gave up, increased by any money you paid. You must keep the records on the old property, as well as on the new property, until the period of limitations expires for the year in which you dispose of the new property in a taxable disposition.

Records for Nontax Purposes

When your records are no longer needed for tax purposes, do not discard them until you check to see if you need to keep them longer for other purposes. For example, your insurance company or creditors may require you to keep them longer than the IRS does.

Bookkeeping System

You must decide whether to use a single-entry or a double-entry bookkeeping system. The single-entry system of bookkeeping is the simplest to maintain, but it may not be suitable for everyone. You may find the doubleentry system better because it has built-in checks and balances to assure accuracy and control.

Single-entry

A single-entry system is based on the income statement (profit or loss statement). It can be a simple and practical system if you are starting a small business. The system records the flow of income and expenses with the use of:

1. A daily summary of cash receipts, and
2. Monthly summaries of cash receipts and disbursements.

Double entry

A double-entry bookkeeping system uses journals and ledgers. Transactions are first entered in a journal and then posted to ledger accounts. These accounts show income, expenses, assets (property a business owns), liabilities (debts of a business), and net worth (excess of assets over liabilities). You close income and expense accounts at the end of each tax year. You keep asset, liability, and net worth accounts open on a permanent basis.

In the double-entry system, each account has a left side for debits and a right side for credits. It is self-balancing because you record every transaction as a debit entry in one account and as a credit entry in another. Under this system, the total debits must equal the total credits after you post the journal entries to the ledger accounts. If the amounts do not balance, you have made an error and you must find and correct it.

An example of a journal entry exhibiting a payment of rent in October is shown next. General Journal Date Description of Entry Debit Credit Oct. 5 Rent expense 780.00 Cash 780.00 Computerized System There are computer software packages you can use for recordkeeping. They can be purchased in many retail stores.

These packages are very helpful and relatively easy to use; they require very little knowledge of bookkeeping and accounting. If you use a computerized system, you must be able to produce enough legible records to support and verify entries made on your return and determine your correct tax liability. To meet this qualification, the machine-sensible records must reconcile with your books and return. These records must provide enough detail to identify the underlying.

You must also keep all machine-sensible records and a complete description of the computerized portion of your recordkeeping system. This documentation must be sufficiently detailed to show the following items.

Functions being performed as the data flows through the system.

Controls used to ensure accurate and reliable processing.

Controls used to prevent the unauthorized addition, alteration, or deletion of retained records.

Charts of accounts and detailed account descriptions.

If you are not sure of what to do, you may want to consult with an accountant before you get started. Depending on how many records you accumulate, if you wait until it is time to file your first business return, you may have a lot of records to put together. It can become overwhelming. It is better to keep daily, weekly and monthly records.

Chapter 5

WHAT IS INCOME?

This chapter primarily explains business income and how to account for it on your tax return, what items are not considered income, and gives guidelines for selected occupations. If there is a connection between any income you receive and your business, the income is business income. A connection exists if it is clear that the payment of income would not have been made if you did not have the business. You can have business income even if you are not involved in the activity on a regular full-time basis. Income from work you do on the side in addition to your regular job can be business income. You report most business income, such as income from selling your products or services, on Schedule C or C-EZ. But you report the income from the sale of business assets, such as land and office buildings, on other forms instead of Schedule C or C-EZ.

Nonemployee Compensation

Business income includes amounts you received in your business that were properly shown on Forms 1099-MISC. This includes amounts reported as nonemployee compensation in box 7 of the form. You can find more information in the instructions on the back of the Form 1099-MISC you received. Business income deduction. Income you report on Schedule C or Schedule C-EZ may be qualified business income and entitle you to a deduction on Form 1040, line 9. Be sure to use the Qualified Business Income Deduction Worksheet in the Instructions for Form 1040 to figure your deduction, if any. This deduction will automatically calculate is you use tax software to prepare your return.

Kinds of Income

You must report on your tax return all income you receive from your business unless it is excluded by law. In most cases, your business income will be in the form of cash, checks, and credit card charges. But business income can be in other forms, such as property or services

Bartering for Property or Services Bartering is an Exchange of Property or Services.

You must include in your gross receipts, at the time received, the fair market value of property or services you receive in exchange for something else. If you exchange services with another person and you both have agreed ahead of time on the value of the services, that value will be accepted as the fair market value unless the value can be shown to be otherwise. Examples are:
1. You are a self-employed lawyer. You perform legal services for a client, a small corporation. In payment for your services, you receive shares of stock in the corporation. You must include the fair market value of the shares in income.
2. You are an artist and create a work of art to compensate your landlord for the rent-free use of your apartment. You must include the fair rental value of the apartment in your gross income.
3. You are a self-employed accountant. Both you and a house painter are members of a barter club, an organization that each year gives its members a directory of members and the services each member provides. Members get in touch with other members directly and bargain for the value of the services to be performed. In return for accounting services you provided for the house painter's business, the house painter painted your home. You must

include in gross receipts the fair market value of the services you received from the house painter. The house painter must include the fair market value of your accounting services in his or her gross receipts.

If you are involved in a bartering transaction, you may have to file either of the following forms.

> Form 1099-B, Proceeds from Broker and Barter Exchange Transactions.
> Form 1099-MISC, Miscellaneous Income.

Real Estate Rents

If you are a real estate dealer who receives income from renting real property or an owner of a hotel, motel, etc., who provides services (maid services, etc.) for guests, report the rental income and expenses on Schedule C or C-EZ. If you are not a real estate dealer or the kind of owner described in the preceding sentence, report the rental income and expenses on Schedule E.

Real Estate Dealer

You are a real estate dealer if you are engaged in the business of selling real estate to customers with the purpose of making a profit from those sales. Rent you receive from real estate held for sale to customers is subject to SE tax. However, rent you receive from real estate held for speculation or investment is not subject to SE tax.

Interest and Dividend Income

Interest and dividends may be considered business income. Interest. Interest received on notes receivable that you have accepted in the ordinary course of business is business income. Interest received on loans is business income if you are in the business of lending money.

Uncollectible Loans

If a loan payable to you becomes uncollectible during the tax year and you use an accrual method of accounting, you must include in gross income interest accrued up to the time the loan became uncollectible. If the accrued interest later becomes uncollectible, you may be able to take a bad debt deduction.

Unstated interest

If little or no interest is charged on an installment sale, you may have to treat a part of each payment as unstated interest.

Dividends

Generally, dividends are business income to dealers in securities. For most sole proprietors and statutory employees, however, dividends are nonbusiness income. If you hold stock as a personal investment separately from your business activity, the dividends from the stock are nonbusiness income. If you receive dividends from business insurance premiums you deducted in an earlier year, you must report all or part of the dividend as business income on your return.

Canceled Debt

The following explains the general rule for including canceled debt in income and the exceptions to the general rule. General Rule Generally, if your debt is canceled or forgiven, other than as a gift or bequest to you, you must include the canceled amount in your gross income for tax purposes. Report the canceled amount on line 6 of Schedule C if you incurred the debt in your business. If the debt is a nonbusiness debt, report the canceled amount on line 21 of Schedule 1 (Form 1040).

Exceptions to the Rule

The following discussion covers some exceptions to the general rule for canceled debt.

Price Reduced After Purchase

If you owe a debt to the seller for property you bought and the seller reduces the amount you owe, you generally do not have income from the reduction. Unless you are bankrupt or insolvent, treat the amount of the reduction as a purchase price adjustment and reduce your basis in the property.

Deductible Debt

You do not realize income from a canceled debt to the extent the payment of the debt would have led to a deduction.

Guidelines for Selected Occupations

This section provides information to determine whether your earnings should be reported on Schedule C (Form 1040) or C-EZ (Form 1040).

Direct Seller

You must report all income you receive as a direct seller on Schedule C or C-EZ. This includes any of the following:
- Income from sales—Payments you receive from customers for products they buy from you.
- Commissions, bonuses, or percentages you receive for sales and the sales of others who work under you.
- Prizes, awards, and gifts you receive from your selling business.

You must report this income regardless of whether it is reported to you on an information return. You are a direct seller if you meet all the following conditions.

You are engaged in one of the following trades or businesses:

Selling or soliciting the sale of consumer products either in a home or other place that is not a permanent retail establishment, or to any buyer on a buy-sell basis or a deposit-commission basis for resale in a home or other place of business that is not a permanent retail establishment.

Delivering or distributing newspapers or shopping news (including any services directly related to that trade or business).

Substantially all your pay (whether paid in cash or not) for services described above is directly related to sales or other output (including performance of services) rather than to the number of hours worked.

Your services are performed under a written contract between you and the person for whom you perform the services, and the contract provides that you will not be treated as an employee for federal tax purposes.

Accounting for Your Income Accounting for your income for income tax purposes differs at times from accounting for financial purposes. This section discusses some of the more common differences that may affect business transactions. Figure your business income on the basis of a tax year and according to your regular method of accounting. If the sale of a product is an income-producing factor in your business, you usually must use inventories to clearly show your income. Dealers in real estate are not allowed to use inventories.

Income paid to a third party. All income you earn is taxable to you. You cannot avoid tax by having the income paid to a third party.

Payment Placed in Escrow

If the buyer of your property places part or all of the purchase price in escrow, you do not include any part of it in gross sales until you actually or constructively receive it. However, upon completion of the terms of the contract and the escrow agreement, you will have taxable income, even if you do not accept the money until the next year.

Sales Returns and Allowances

Credits you allow customers for returned merchandise and any other allowances you make on sales are deductions from gross sales in figuring net sales.

Advance Payments

Special rules dealing with an accrual method of accounting for payments received in advance are discussed in chapter about the accrual method

Insurance Proceeds

If you receive insurance or another type of reimbursement for a casualty or theft loss, you must subtract it from the loss when you figure your deduction. You cannot deduct the reimbursed part of a casualty or theft loss.

Chapter 6

BUSINESS DEDUCTIONS

As a business owner you can deduct all expenses that are both ordinary and necessary incurred in operating your business. An ordinary expense is one that is common and accepted in your field of business. A necessary expense is one that is helpful and appropriate for your business. Below I will list some of the most used business expenses. There are certainly industries that will have expenses that are not listed here. Be sure to have proof of payment for all expenses and documentation that shows how it is an expense for operating your business.

BAD DEBTS

You may be able to deduct business bad debts as an expense on your business tax return. A business bad debt is a loss from the worthlessness of a debt that was either of the following:

Created or acquired in your business
Closely related to your business when it became partly or totally worthless

A debt is closely related to your business if your primary motive for incurring the debt is a business reason. Business bad debts are mainly the result of credit sales to customers. They can result from loans to suppliers, clients, employees or distributors.

Car and Truck Expenses

If you use your car or truck in your business, you may be able to deduct the costs of operating and maintaining your vehicle. You also may be able to deduct other costs of local transportation and traveling away from home overnight on business.

Local Transportation Expenses

Local transportation expenses include the ordinary and necessary costs of all the following.

- Getting from one workplace to another in the course of your business or profession when you are traveling within the city or general area that is your tax home.
- Visiting clients or customers.
- Going to a business meeting away from your regular workplace.
- Getting from your home to a temporary workplace when you have one or more regular places of work. These temporary workplaces can be either within the area of your tax home or outside that area. Local business transportation does not include expenses you have while traveling away from home overnight. Those expenses are deductible as travel expenses. However, if you use your car while traveling away from home overnight, use the rules in this section to figure your car expense deduction. Generally, your tax home is your regular place of business, regardless of where you maintain your family home. It includes the entire city or general area in which your business or work is located.

Example. You operate a printing business out of rented office space. You use your van to deliver completed jobs to your customers. You can deduct the cost of round-trip transportation between your customers and your print shop. You cannot deduct the costs of driving your car or truck between your home and your main or regular workplace. These costs are personal commuting expenses.

Office in the home. Your workplace can be your home if you have an office in your home that qualifies as your principal place of business.

Methods for Deducting Car and Truck Expenses

For local transportation or overnight travel by car or truck, you generally can use one of the following methods to figure your expenses.
- Standard mileage rate.
- Actual expenses.

Standard Mileage Rate

You may be able to use the standard mileage rate to figure the deductible costs of operating your car, van, pickup, or panel truck for business purposes. For 2018, the standard mileage rate is 54.5 cents per mile. If you choose to use the standard mileage rate for a year, you cannot deduct your actual expenses for that year except for business-related parking fees and tolls.

If you want to use the standard mileage rate for a car or truck you own, you must choose to use it in the first year the car is available for use in your business. In later years, you can choose to use either the standard mileage rate or actual expenses. If you use the standard mileage rate for a car you lease, you must choose to use it for the entire lease period (including renewals). Standard mileage rate not allowed.

You cannot use the standard mileage rate if you:
1. Operate five or more cars at the same time;
2. Claimed a depreciation deduction using any method other than straight line, for example, ACRS or MACRS;
3. Claimed a section 179 deduction on the car;
4. Claimed the special depreciation allowance on the car;
5. Claimed actual car expenses for a car you leased; or
6. Are a rural mail carrier who received a qualified reimbursement. Parking fees and tolls. In addition to using the standard mileage rate, you can deduct any business-related parking fees and

tolls. (Parking fees you pay to park your car at your place of work are nondeductible commuting expenses.) Actual expenses. If you do not choose to use the standard mileage rate, you may be able to deduct your actual car or truck expenses.

If you qualify to use both methods, figure your deduction both ways to see which gives you a larger deduction. Actual car expenses include the costs of the following items

- Depreciation
- Lease payments
- Registration
- Garage rent
- Licenses
- Repairs
- Gas Oil
- Tires
- Insurance
- Parking Fees
- Tolls

If you use your vehicle for both business and personal purposes, you must divide your expenses between business and personal use. You can divide your expenses based on the miles driven for each purpose. **Example**. You are the sole proprietor of a flower shop. You drove your van 20,000 miles during the year. 16,000 miles were for delivering flowers to customers and 4,000 miles were for personal use (including commuting miles). You can claim only 80% (16,000 ÷ 20,000) of the cost of operating your van as a business expense.

Reimbursing Your Employees for Expenses

You generally can deduct the amount you reimburse your employees for car and truck expenses. The reimbursement you deduct and the way you deduct it depend in part on whether you reimburse the expenses under an accountable plan or a nonaccountable plan.

Depreciation

If property you acquire to use in your business is expected to last more than 1 year, you generally cannot deduct the entire cost as a business expense in the year you acquire it. You must spread the cost over more than 1 tax year and deduct part of it each year on Schedule C. This method of deducting the cost of business property is called depreciation.

Depreciation is one of the more complex tax deductions for business as there are several options you can choose, and each will render a different amount of depreciation for the present year and the years going forward.

What property can be depreciated? You can depreciate property if it meets all the following requirements.
- It must be property you own.
- It must be used in business or held to produce income. You never can depreciate inventory.
- It must have a useful life that extends substantially beyond the year it is placed in service.
- It must have a determinable useful life, which means that it must be something that wears out, decays, gets used up, becomes obsolete, or loses its value from natural causes.

You never can depreciate the cost of land because land does not wear out, become obsolete, or get used up.
- It must not be excepted property. This includes property placed in service and disposed of in the same year. Repairs. In general, you do not depreciate the costs of repairs or maintenance if they do not improve your property. Instead, you deduct these amounts on line 21 of Schedule C or line 2 of Schedule C-EZ. Improvements are amounts paid for betterments to your property, restorations of your property, or work that adapts your property to a new or different use.

Election to capitalize repair and maintenance costs that do not improve your property. You can make an election to treat certain repairs or replacements in your trade or business as improvements subject to depreciation. This election is available if you treat these amounts as capital expenditures on your books and records regularly used in computing your income and expense.

Depreciation Method

The method for depreciating most business and investment property placed in service after 1986 is called the Modified Accelerated Cost Recovery System (MACRS).

Section 179 Deduction

You can elect to deduct a limited amount of the cost of certain depreciable property in the year you place the property in service. This deduction is known as the "section 179 deduction." The maximum amount you can elect to deduct during 2018 generally is $1 million (higher limits apply to certain property). This limit generally is reduced by the amount by which the cost of the property placed in service during the tax year exceeds $2,500,000. The total amount of depreciation (including the section 179 deduction) you can take for a passenger automobile you use in your business and first place in service in 2018 is $10,000 ($18,000 if you take the special depreciation allowance for qualified passenger automobiles placed in service in 2018).

Special rules apply to trucks and vans. For more information, see IRS Pub. 946. It explains what property qualifies for the deduction, what limits apply to the deduction, and when and how to recapture the deduction. Your section 179 election for the cost of any sport utility vehicle (SUV) and certain other vehicles is limited to $25,000. For more information, see the Instructions for Form 4562 or Pub. 946.

Listed Property

You must follow special rules and recordkeeping requirements when depreciating listed property. Listed property includes any of the following.

- Most passenger automobiles.

- Most other property used for transportation.
- Any property of a type generally used for entertainment, recreation, or amusement.

Use Form 4562, Depreciation and Amortization, if you are claiming any of the following.

- Depreciation on property placed in service during the current tax year.
- A section 179 deduction.
- Depreciation on any listed property (regardless of when it was placed in service).

If you are required to use Form 4562, you must file Schedule C. You cannot use Schedule C-EZ.

Employees' Pay

You generally can deduct on Schedule C the pay you give your employees for the services they perform for your business. The pay may be in cash, property, or services. To be deductible, your employees' pay must be an ordinary and necessary expense and you must pay or incur it in the tax year. In addition, the pay must meet both the following tests.

- The pay must be reasonable.
- The pay must be for services performed.

You cannot deduct your own salary or any personal withdrawals you make from your business. As a sole proprietor, you are not an employee of the business. If you had employees during the year, you must use Schedule C. You cannot use Schedule C-EZ.

Kinds of Pay

Some of the ways you may provide pay to your employees are listed below

- Awards.
- Bonuses.
- Education expenses.
- Fringe benefits.
- Loans or advances you do not expect the employee to repay if they are for personal services performed.
- Property you transfer to an employee as payment for services.
- Reimbursements for employee business expenses.
- Sick pay.
- Vacation pay.

Fringe Benefits

A fringe benefit is a form of pay for the performance of services. The following are examples of fringe benefits.
- Benefits under qualified employee benefit programs.
- Meals and lodging.
- The use of a car.
- Flights on airplanes.
- Discounts on property or services.

Employee benefit programs include the following.
- Accident and health plans.
- Adoption assistance.
- Cafeteria plans.
- Dependent care assistance.
- Educational assistance.
- Group-term life insurance coverage.
- Welfare benefit funds.

You generally can deduct the cost of fringe benefits you provide on your Schedule C in whatever category the cost falls. For example, if you allow an employee to use a car or other property you lease, deduct the cost of the lease as a rent or lease expense. If you own the property, include your deduction for its cost or other basis as a section 179 deduction or a depreciation deduction.

You may be able to exclude all, or part of the fringe benefits you provide from your employees' wages.

Insurance

You generally can deduct premiums you pay for the following kinds of insurance related to your business.
1. Fire, theft, flood, or similar insurance.
2. Credit insurance that covers losses from business bad debts.
3. Group hospitalization and medical insurance for employees, including long-term care insurance.
4. Liability insurance.
5. Malpractice insurance that covers your personal liability for professional negligence resulting in injury or damage to patients or clients.
6. Workers' compensation insurance set by state law that covers any claims for bodily injuries or job-related diseases suffered by employees in your business, regardless of fault.
The type and rule above prints on all proofs including departmental reproduction proofs. MUST be removed before printing.
7. Contributions to a state unemployment insurance fund are deductible as taxes if they are considered taxes under state law.
8. Overhead insurance that pays for business overhead expenses you have during long periods of disability caused by your injury or sickness.
9. Car and other vehicle insurance that covers vehicles used in your business for liability, damages, and other losses. If you operate a vehicle partly for personal use, deduct only the part of the insurance premium that applies to the business use of the vehicle. If you use the standard mileage rate to figure your car expenses, you cannot deduct any car insurance premiums.
10. Life insurance covering your employees if you are not directly or indirectly the beneficiary under the contract.
11. Business interruption insurance that pays for lost profits if your business is shut down due to a fire or other cause.

Nondeductible Premiums

You cannot deduct premiums on the following kinds of insurance.

1. Self-insurance reserve funds. You cannot deduct amounts credited to a reserve set up for self-insurance. This applies even if you cannot get business insurance coverage for certain business risks. However, your actual losses may be deductible.

2. Loss of earnings. You cannot deduct premiums for a policy that pays for your lost earnings due to sickness or disability

3. Certain life insurance and annuities.

a. For contracts issued before June 9, 1997, you cannot deduct the premiums on a life insurance policy covering you, an employee, or any person with a financial interest in your business if you are directly or indirectly a beneficiary of the policy. You are included among possible beneficiaries of the policy if the policy owner is obligated to repay a loan from you using the proceeds of the policy. A person has a financial interest in your business if the person is an owner or part owner of the business or has lent money to the business.

b. For contracts issued after June 8, 1997, you generally cannot deduct the premiums on any life insurance policy, endowment contract, or annuity contract if you are directly or indirectly a beneficiary. The disallowance applies without regard to whom the policy covers.

4. Insurance to secure a loan. If you take out a policy on your life or on the life of another person with a financial interest in your business to get or protect a business loan, you cannot deduct the premiums as a business expense. Nor can you deduct the premiums as interest on business loans or as an expense of financing loans. In the event of death, the proceeds of the policy are not taxed as income even if they are used to liquidate the debt.

Self-employed Health Insurance Deduction

You may be able to deduct the amount you paid for medical and dental insurance and qualified long-term care insurance for you and your family. How to figure the deduction. Generally, you can use the worksheet in the Instructions for Form 1040 to figure your deduction. However, if any of the following apply, you must use the worksheet in chapter 6 of Pub. 535.

- You have more than one source of income subject to self-employment tax.
- You file Form 2555 or Form 2555-EZ (relating to foreign earned income).
- You are using amounts paid for qualified long-term care insurance to figure the deduction. Use Pub. 974 instead of the worksheet in the Instructions for Form 1040 if the insurance plan established, or considered to be established, under your business was obtained through the Health Insurance Marketplace and you are claiming the premium tax credit.

Prepayment

You cannot deduct expenses in advance, even if you pay them in advance. This rule applies to any expense paid far enough in advance to, in effect, create an asset with a useful life extending substantially beyond the end of the current tax year. **Example.** In 2018, you signed a 3-year insurance contract. Even though you paid the premiums for 2018, 2019, and 2020 when you signed the contract, you can only deduct the premium for 2018 on your 2018 tax return. You can deduct in 2019 and 2020 the premium allocable to those years.

Interest

You generally can deduct as a business expense some or all interest you pay or accrue during the tax year on debts related to your business. Interest relates to your business if you use the proceeds of the loan for a business expense. It does not matter what type of property secures the loan. You can deduct interest on a debt only if you meet all of the following requirements.
- You are legally liable for that debt.
- Both you and the lender intend that the debt be repaid.
- You and the lender have a true debtor-creditor relationship. Certain taxpayers are required to limit their business interest expense deduction.

You cannot deduct on Schedule C or C-EZ the interest you paid on personal loans. If a loan is part business and part personal, you must divide the interest between the personal part and the business part. **Example.** In 2018, you paid $600 interest on a car loan. During 2018, you used the car 60% for business and 40% for personal purposes. You are claiming actual expenses on the car. You can only deduct $360 (60% × $600) for 2018 on Schedule C or C-EZ. The remaining interest of $240 is a nondeductible personal expense

Legal and Professional Fees

Legal and professional fees, such as fees charged by accountants, that are ordinary and necessary expenses directly related to operating your business are deductible on Schedule C or C-EZ. However, you usually cannot deduct legal fees you pay to acquire business assets. Add them to the basis of the property. If the fees include payments for work of a personal nature (such as making a will), you can take a business deduction only for the part of the fee related to your business.

You can also claim a business deduction for amounts paid or incurred in resolving asserted tax deficiencies for your business operated as a sole proprietor.

Tax Preparation Fees

You can deduct on Schedule C or C-EZ the cost of preparing that part of your tax return relating to your business as a sole proprietor or statutory employee. You also can deduct on Schedule C or C-EZ the amount you pay or incur in resolving asserted tax deficiencies for your business as a sole proprietor or statutory employee.

Pension Plans

You can set up and maintain the following small business retirement plans for yourself and your employees.

- SEP (Simplified Employee Pension) plans.

- SIMPLE (Savings Incentive Match Plan for Employees) plans.
- Qualified plans (including Keogh or H.R. 10 plans).

SEP, SIMPLE, and qualified plans offer you and your employees a tax favored way to save for retirement. You can deduct contributions you make to the plan for your employees on line 19 of Schedule C. If you are a sole proprietor, you can deduct contributions you make to the plan for yourself on line 28 of Schedule 1 (Form 1040). You also can deduct trustees' fees if contributions to the plan.

Rent Expense

Rent is any amount you pay for the use of property you do not own. In general, you can deduct rent as a business expense only if the rent is for property you use in your business. If you have or will receive equity in or title to the property, you cannot deduct the rent.

You cannot take a rental deduction for unreasonable rents. Ordinarily, the issue of reasonableness arises only if you and the lessor are related. Rent paid to a related person is reasonable if it is the same amount you would pay to a stranger for use of the same property. Rent is not unreasonable just because it is figured as a percentage of gross receipts. Related persons include members of your immediate family, including brothers and sisters (either whole or half), your spouse, ancestors, and lineal descendants.

Rent on Your Home

If you rent your home and use part of it as your place of business, you may be able to deduct the rent you pay for that part. You must meet the requirements for business use of your home.

Rent Paid in Advance

Generally, rent paid in your business is deductible in the year paid or accrued. If you pay rent in advance, you can deduct only the amount that applies to your use of the rented property during the tax year. You can deduct the rest of your payment only over the period to which it applies.

Taxes

You can deduct on Schedule C or C-EZ various federal, state, local, and foreign taxes directly attributable to your business.

as an employer to a state unemployment compensation fund or to a state disability benefit fund. Deduct these payments as taxes.

Self-employment Tax

You can deduct one-half of your self-employment tax on line 27 of Schedule 1 (Form 1040).

Personal Property Tax

You can deduct on Schedule C or C-EZ any tax imposed by a state or local government on personal property used in your business. You also can deduct registration fees for the right to use property within a state or local area. **Example.** May and Julius Winter drove their car 7,000 business miles out of a total of 10,000 miles. They had to pay $25 for their annual state license tags and $20 for their city registration sticker. They also paid $235 in city personal property tax on the car, for a total of $280. They are claiming their actual car expenses. Because they used the car 70% for business, they can deduct 70% of the $280, or $196, as a business expense.

Real Estate Taxes

You can deduct on Schedule C or C-EZ the real estate taxes you pay on your business property. Deductible real estate taxes are any state, local, or foreign taxes on real estate levied for the general public welfare. The taxing authority must assess these taxes uniformly at a like rate on all real property under its jurisdiction, and the proceeds must be for general community or governmental purposes.

Special Rules

Special rules apply for the following:

- Taxes for local benefits, such as those for sidewalks, streets, water mains, and sewer lines.
- Real estate taxes when you buy or sell property during the year.
- Real estate taxes if you use an accrual method of accounting and choose to accrue real estate tax related to a definite period ratably over that period.

Sales Tax

Treat any sales tax you pay on a service or on the purchase or use of property as part of the cost of the service or property. If the service or the cost or use of the property is a deductible business expense, you can deduct the tax as part of that service or cost. If the property is merchandise bought for resale, the sales tax is part of the cost of the merchandise. If the property is depreciable, add the sales tax to the basis for depreciation.

Basis of Assets

Do not deduct state and local sales taxes imposed on the buyer that you must collect and pay over to the state or local government. Do not include these taxes in gross receipts or sales.

Excise Taxes

You can deduct on Schedule C or C-EZ all excise taxes that are ordinary and necessary expenses of carrying on your business.

Fuel Taxes

Taxes on gasoline, diesel fuel, and other motor fuels you use in your business are usually included as part of the cost of the fuel. Do not deduct these taxes as a separate item. You may be entitled to a credit or refund for federal excise tax you paid on fuels used for certain purposes.

Travel and Meals

These are the ordinary and necessary expenses of traveling away from home for your business. You are traveling away from home if both the following conditions are met.
1. Your duties require you to be away from the general area of your tax home substantially longer than an ordinary day's work.
2. You need to get sleep or rest to meet the demands of your work while away from home. Generally, your tax home is your regular place of business, regardless of where you maintain your family home. It includes the entire city or general area in which your business is located. The following is a brief discussion of the expenses you can deduct.

Transportation. You can deduct the cost of travel by airplane, train, bus, or car between your home and your business destination. Taxi, commuter bus, and limousine. You can deduct fares for these and other types of transportation between the airport or station and your hotel, or between the hotel and your work location away from home.

Baggage and shipping. You can deduct the cost of sending baggage and sample or display material between your regular and temporary work locations.

Car or truck. You can deduct the costs of operating and maintaining your vehicle when traveling away from home on business. You can deduct actual expenses or the standard mileage rate, as well as business-related tolls and parking. If you rent a car while away from home on business, you can deduct only the business-use portion of the expenses.

Meals and lodging. You can deduct the cost of meals and lodging if your business trip is overnight or long enough that you need to stop for sleep or rest to properly perform your duties. You can use actual expenses or standard meal allowance to calculate your deduction. In most cases, you can deduct only 50% of your meal expenses.

Cleaning. You can deduct the costs of dry cleaning and laundry while on your business trip.   **Telephone**. You can deduct the cost of business calls while on your business trip, including business communication by fax machine or other communication devices.

Tips. You can deduct the tips you pay for any expense in this list. More information. For more information about travel expenses.

Reimbursing Your Employees for Expense

You generally can deduct the amount you reimburse your employees for travel and meal expenses. The reimbursement you deduct and the way you deduct it depend in part on whether you reimburse the expenses under an accountable plan or a nonaccountable plan.

Reimbursement of Travel and Non-Entertainment Related Meals

The following discussion explains how to handle any reimbursements or allowances you may provide to your employees under a reimbursement or allowance arrangement for travel and non-entertainment related meals expenses. If you are self-employed and report your income and expenses on Schedule C (Form 1040) or Schedule C-EZ (Form 1040). To be deductible for tax purposes, expenses incurred for travel and non-entertainment related meals must be ordinary and necessary expenses incurred while carrying on your trade or business. Generally, you also must show that non-entertainment related meals expenses are directly related to, or associated with, the conduct of your trade or business.

Reimbursements

A "reimbursement or allowance arrangement" provides for payment of advances, reimbursements, and allowances for travel and non-entertainment

related meals expenses incurred by your employees during the ordinary course of business. If the expenses are substantiated, you can deduct the allowable amount on your tax return. Because of differences between accounting methods and tax law, the amount you can deduct for tax purposes may not be the same as the amount you deduct on your business books and records. For example, you can deduct 100% of the cost of meals on your business books and records. However, only 50% of these costs are allowed by law as a tax deduction. How you deduct a business expense under a reimbursement or allowance arrangement depends on whether you have:
- An accountable plan, or
- A nonaccountable plan.

If you reimburse these expenses under an accountable plan, deduct them as travel and non-entertainment related meals expenses. If you reimburse these expenses under a nonaccountable plan, report the reimbursements as wages on Form W-2, and deduct them as wages on the appropriate line of your tax return. If you make a single payment to your employees and it includes both wages and an expense reimbursement, you must specify the amount of the reimbursement and report it accordingly.

Accountable Plans

An accountable plan requires your employees to meet all the following requirements. Each employee must:

1. Have paid or incurred deductible expenses while performing services as your employee,
2. Adequately account to you for these expenses within a reasonable period, and
3. Return any excess reimbursement or allowance within a reasonable period.

An arrangement under which you advance money to employees is treated as meeting (3) above only if the following requirements are also met.
- The advance is reasonably calculated not to exceed the amount of anticipated expenses.
- You make the advance within a reasonable period of your employee paying or incurring the expense.

If any expenses reimbursed under this arrangement aren't substantiated, or an excess under this arrangement aren't substantiated, or an excess reimbursement isn't returned within a reasonable period by an employee, you cannot treat these expenses as reimbursed under an accountable plan. Instead, treat the reimbursed expenses as paid under a nonaccountable plan, discussed later.

Adequate Accounting

Your employees must adequately account to you for their travel and non-entertainment related meals expenses. They must give you documentary evidence of their travel, mileage, and other employee business expenses. This evidence should include items such as receipts, along with either a statement of expenses, an account book, a day-planner, or similar record in which the employee entered each expense at or near the time the expense was incurred.

Excess Reimbursement or Allowance

An excess reimbursement or allowance is any amount you pay to an employee that is more than the business-related expenses for which the employee adequately accounted. The employee must return any excess reimbursement or other expense allowance to you within a reasonable period. A reasonable period of time depends on the facts and circumstances. Generally, actions that take place within the times specified in the following list will be treated as taking place within a reasonable period.

1. You give an advance within 30 days of the time the employee pays or incurs the expense.
2. Your employees adequately account for their expenses within 60 days after the expenses were paid or incurred.
3. Your employees return any excess reimbursement within 120 days after the expenses were paid or incurred.
4. You give a periodic statement (at least quarterly) to your employees that asks them to either return or adequately account for outstanding advances and they comply within 120 days of the date of the statement.

You can claim a deduction for travel and non-entertainment related meals expenses if you reimburse your employees for these expenses under an accountable plan. Generally, the amount you can deduct for non-entertainment related meals is subject to a 50% limit. If you are a sole proprietor, or are filing as a single member limited liability company, deduct the travel reimbursement on line 24a and the deductible part of the non-entertainment related meals reimbursement on line 24b, Schedule C (Form 1040), or line 2, Schedule C-EZ (Form 1040).

If you are filing an income tax return for a corporation, include the reimbursement on the Other deductions line of Form 1120. If you are filing any other business income tax return, such as a partnership or S corporation return, deduct the reimbursement on the appropriate line of the return as provided in the instructions for that return.

Per Diem and Car Allowances You can reimburse your employees under an accountable plan based on travel days, miles, or some other fixed allowance. In these cases, your employee is considered to have accounted to you for the expense that doesn't exceed the rates established by the federal government. Your employee must substantiate to you the other elements of the expense, such as time, place, and business purpose.

Federal rate. The federal rate can be figured using any one of the following methods.

1. For car expenses:
a. The standard mileage rate.
b. A fixed and variable rate (FAVR).

2. For per diem amounts:
a. The regular federal per diem rate
b. The standard meal allowance.
c. The high-low rate.

Car allowance. Your employee is considered to have accounted to you for car expenses that do not exceed the standard mileage rate. Beginning in 2018, the standard business mileage rate is 54.5 cents per mile. You can choose to reimburse your employees using an FAVR allowance. This is an allowance that includes a combination of payments covering fixed and variable costs, such as a cents-per-mile rate to cover your employees' variable operating costs (such as gas, oil, etc.) plus a flat amount to cover your employees' fixed costs (such as depreciation, insurance, etc.).

Per diem allowance. If your employee actually substantiates to you the other elements of the expenses reimbursed using the per diem allowance, how you report and deduct the allowance depends on whether the allowance is for lodging and meal expenses or for meal expenses only and whether the allowance is more than the federal rate.

Regular federal per diem rate. The regular federal per diem rate is the highest amount the federal government will pay to its employees while away from home on travel. It has the following two components.

1. Lodging expense.
2. Meal and incidental expense (M&IE). The rates are different for different locations. See GSA.gov/perdiem for the per diem rates in the continental United States.

Standard meal allowance. The federal rate for M&IE is the standard meal allowance. You can pay only an M&IE allowance to employees who travel away from home if:

- You pay the employee for actual expenses for lodging based on receipts submitted to you,
- You provide for the lodging,
- You pay for the actual expense of the lodging directly to the provider,
- You don't have a reasonable belief that lodging expenses were incurred by the employee, or
- The allowance is figured on a basis like the one used in figuring the employee's wages (that is, number of hours worked, or miles traveled).

High-low method. This is a simplified method of figuring the federal per diem rate for travel within the continental United States. It eliminates the need to keep a current list of the per diem rate for each city. Under the high-low method, the per diem amount for travel during January through September of 2018 is $284 ($68 for M&IE) for certain high-cost locations. All other areas have a per diem amount of $191 ($57 for M&IE). The high-cost localities eligible for the higher per diem amount under the high-low method are listed in Notice 2018-77, available at IRS.gov. Effective October 1, 2018, the per diem rate for high-cost locations increased to $287 ($71 for M&IE). The rate for all other locations increased to $195 ($60 for M&IE). For October, November, and

December 2018, you can either continue to use the rates described in the preceding paragraph or change to the new rates. However, you must use the same rate for all employees reimbursed under the high-low method. Go to www.GSA.gov/perdiem for the current per diem rates for all locations.

Reporting per diem and car allowances. The following discussion explains how to report per diem and car allowances. How you report them depends on how the allowance compares to the federal rate. If your allowance for the employee is less than or equal to the appropriate federal rate, that allowance isn't included as part of the employee's pay in box 1 of the employee's Form W-2. Deduct the allowance as travel expenses (including meals that may be subject to the 50% limit, discussed later).

See How to deduct under Accountable Plans, earlier.

Allowance more than the federal rate. If your employee's allowance is more than the appropriate federal rate, you must report the allowance as two separate items. Include the allowance amount up to the federal rate in box 12 (code L) of the employee's Form W-2. Deduct it as travel expenses (as explained above). This part of the allowance is treated as reimbursed under an accountable plan. Include the amount that is more than the federal rate in box 1 (and in boxes 3 and 5 if they apply) of the Form W-2. Deduct it as wages subject to income tax withholding, social security, Medicare, and federal unemployment taxes. This part of the allowance is treated as reimbursed under a nonaccountable plan as explained later under Nonaccountable Plans.

Meals and Entertainment Under an accountable plan, you can generally deduct only 50% of any otherwise deductible business-related meal and entertainment expenses you reimburse your employees. The deduction limit applies even if you reimburse them for 100% of the expenses.

Application of the 50% limit. The 50% deduction limit applies to reimbursements you make to your employees for expenses they incur for meals while traveling away from home on business and for entertaining business customers at your place of business, a restaurant, or another location. It applies to expenses incurred at a business convention or reception, business meeting, or business luncheon at a club. The deduction limit may also apply to meals you furnish on your premises to your employees.

Related expenses. Taxes and tips relating to a meal or entertainment activity you reimburse to your employee under an accountable plan are included in the amount subject to the 50% limit. Reimbursements you make for expenses, such as cover charges for admission to a nightclub, rent paid for a room to hold a dinner or cocktail party, or the amount you pay for parking at a sports arena, are all subject to the 50% limit. However, the cost of transportation to and from an otherwise allowable business meal or a business-related entertainment activity isn't subject to the 50% limit.

Amount subject to 50% limit. If you provide your employees with a per diem allowance only for meal and incidental expenses, the amount treated as an expense for food and beverages is the lesser of the following.

- The per diem allowance.
- The federal rate for M&IE.

If you provide your employees with a per diem allowance that covers lodging, meals, and incidental expenses, you must treat an amount equal to the federal M&IE rate for the area of travel as an expense for food and beverages. If the per diem allowance you provide is less than the federal per diem rate for the area of travel, you can treat 40% of the per diem allowance as the amount for food and beverages.

Meal expenses when subject to "hours of service" limits. You can deduct 80% of the cost of reimbursed meals your employees consume while away from their tax home on business during, or incident to, any period subject to the Department of Transportation's "hours of service" limits. See Pub. 463 for a detailed discussion of individuals subject to the Department of Transportation's "hours of service" limits.

De minimis (minimal) fringe benefit. The 50% limit doesn't apply to an expense for food or beverage that is excluded from the gross income of an employee because it is a de minimis fringe benefit.

Company cafeteria or executive dining room. The cost of food and beverages you provide primarily to your employees on your business premises is deductible. This includes the cost of maintaining the facilities for providing the food and beverages. These expenses are subject to the 50% limit unless they qualify as a de minimis fringe benefit, as mentioned, or unless they are compensation to your employees.

Employee activities. The expense of providing recreational, social, or similar activities (including the use of a facility) for your employees is deductible and isn't subject to the 50% limit. The benefit must be primarily for your employees who aren't highly compensated. For this purpose, a highly compensated employee is an employee who meets either of the following requirements.

1. Owned a 5% or more interest in the business during the year or the preceding year. An employee is treated as owning any interest owned by his or her brother, sister, spouse, ancestors, and lineal descendants.

2. Received more than $80,000 in pay for the preceding year.

You can choose to include only employees who were also in the top 20% of employees when ranked by pay for the preceding year. For example, the expenses for food, beverages, and entertainment for a company-wide picnic aren't subject to the 50% limit.

Meals or entertainment treated as compensation. The 50% limit doesn't apply to either of the following.

1. Expenses for meals or entertainment that you treat as:

Compensation to an employee who was the recipient of the meals or entertainment, and wages subject to withholding of federal income tax.

2. Expenses for meals or entertainment if:

A recipient of the meals or entertainment who isn't your employee has to include the expenses in gross income as compensation for services or as a prize or award; and

You include that amount on a Form 1099-MISC issued to the recipient, if a Form 1099-MISC is required.

Sales of meals or entertainment. You can deduct the cost of meals or entertainment (including the use of facilities) you sell to the public. For example, if you run a nightclub, your expense for the entertainment you furnish to your customers, such as a floor show, is a business expense that is fully deductible. The 50% limit doesn't apply to this expense.

Providing meals or entertainment to general public to promote goodwill. You can deduct the cost of providing meals, entertainment, or recreational facilities to the general public as a means of advertising or promoting goodwill in the community. The 50% limit doesn't apply to this expense.

Director, stockholder, or employee meetings. You can deduct entertainment expenses directly related to business meetings of your employees, partners, stockholders, agents, or directors. You can provide some minor social activities, but the main purpose of the meeting must be your company's business. These expenses are subject to the 50% limit.

Trade association meetings. You can deduct expenses directly related to and necessary for attending business meetings or conventions of certain tax-exempt organizations. These organizations include business leagues, chambers of commerce, real estate boards, and trade and professional associations.

Nonaccountable Plans

A nonaccountable plan is an arrangement that doesn't meet the requirements for an accountable plan. All amounts paid, or treated as paid, under a nonaccountable plan are reported as wages on Form W-2. The payments are subject to income tax withholding, social security, Medicare, and federal unemployment taxes. You can deduct the reimbursement as compensation or wages only to the extent it meets the deductibility tests for employees' pay.

Deduct the allowable amount as compensation or wages on the appropriate line of your income tax return, as provided in its instructions.

Miscellaneous Expenses

In addition to travel, meal, and entertainment expenses, there are other expenses you can deduct.

Advertising expenses. You generally can deduct reasonable advertising expenses that are directly related to your business activities. Generally, you can't deduct amounts paid to influence legislation (for example, lobbying). You can usually deduct as a business expense the cost of institutional or goodwill advertising to keep your name before the public if it relates to business you reasonably expect to gain in the future. For example, the cost of advertising that encourages people to contribute to the Red Cross, to buy U.S. Savings Bonds, or to participate in similar causes is usually deductible.

Anticipated liabilities. Anticipated liabilities or reserves for anticipated liabilities aren't deductible. For example, assume you sold 1-year TV service contracts this year totaling $50,000. From experience, you know you will have expenses of about $15,000 in the coming year for these contracts. You can't deduct any of the $15,000 this year by charging expenses to a reserve or liability account. You can deduct your expenses only when you actually pay or accrue them, depending on your accounting method.

Bribes and kickbacks. Engaging in the payment of bribes or kickbacks is a serious criminal matter. Such activity could result in criminal prosecution. Any payments that appear to have been made, either directly or indirectly, to an official or employee of any government or an agency or instrumentality of any government aren't deductible for tax purposes and are in violation of the law. Payments paid directly or indirectly to a person in violation of any federal or state law (but only if that state law is generally enforced, defined below) that provides for a criminal penalty or for the loss of a license or privilege to engage in a trade or business aren't allowed as a deduction for tax purposes. Meaning of "generally enforced." A state law is considered generally enforced unless it is never enforced or enforced only for infamous persons or persons whose violations are extraordinarily flagrant. For example, a state law is generally enforced unless proper reporting of a violation of the law results in enforcement only under unusual circumstances.

Kickbacks. A kickback is a payment for referring a client, patient, or customer. The common kickback situation occurs when money or property is given to someone as payment for influencing a third party to purchase from, use the services of, or otherwise deal with the person who pays the kickback. In many cases, the person whose business is being sought or enjoyed by the person who pays the kickback isn't aware of the payment. For example, the Yard Corporation is in the business of repairing ships. It returns 10% of the repair bills as kickbacks to the captains and chief officers of the vessels it repairs. Although this practice is considered an ordinary and necessary expense of getting business, it is clearly a violation of a state law that is generally enforced. These expenditures aren't deductible for tax purposes, whether or not the owners of the shipyard are subsequently prosecuted.

Charitable contributions. Cash payments to an organization, charitable or otherwise, may be deductible as business expenses if the payments aren't charitable contributions or gifts and are directly related to your business. If the payments are charitable contributions or gifts, you can't deduct them as business expenses. However, corporations (other than S corporations) can deduct charitable contributions on their income tax returns, subject to limitations. See the Instructions for Form 1120 for more information.

Sole proprietors, partners in a partnership, or shareholders in an S corporation may be able to deduct charitable contributions made by their business on Schedule A (Form 1040). Example. You paid $15 to a local church for a half-page ad in a program for a concert it is sponsoring. The purpose of the ad was to encourage readers to buy your products. Your payment isn't a charitable contribution. You can deduct it as an advertising expense. Example. You made a $100,000 donation to a committee organized by the local Chamber of Commerce to bring a convention to your city, intended to increase business activity, including yours. Your payment isn't a charitable contribution. You can deduct it as a business expense.

Club dues and membership fees. Generally, you can't deduct amounts paid or incurred for membership in any club organized for business, pleasure, recreation, or any other social purpose. This includes country clubs, golf and athletic clubs, hotel clubs, sporting clubs, airline clubs, and clubs operated to provide meals under circumstances generally considered to be conducive to business discussions. Exception.

The following organizations aren't treated as clubs organized for business, pleasure, recreation, or other social purpose unless one of the main purposes is to conduct entertainment activities for members or their guests or to provide members or their guests with access to entertainment facilities.

Boards of trade. Business leagues.

Chambers of commerce

Civic or public service organizations.

Professional organizations such as bar associations and medical associations.

Real estate boards.

Trade associations.

Credit card convenience fees. Credit card companies charge a fee to businesses who accept their cards. This fee when paid or incurred by the business can be deducted as a business expense. Damages recovered. Special rules apply to compensation you receive for damages sustained as a result of patent infringement, breach of contract or fiduciary duty, or antitrust violations. You must include this compensation in your income. However, you may be able to take a special deduction. The deduction applies only to amounts recovered for actual economic injury, not any additional amount. The deduction is the smaller of the following.

- The amount you received or accrued for damages in the tax year reduced by the amount you paid or incurred in the year to recover that amount.
- Your losses from the injury you haven't deducted. Demolition expenses or losses. Amounts paid or incurred to demolish a structure aren't deductible. These amounts are added to the basis of the land where the demolished structure was located. Any loss for the remaining undepreciated basis of a demolished structure wouldn't be recognized until the property is disposed of.

Education expenses. Ordinary and necessary expenses paid for the cost of the education and training of your employees are deductible. You can also deduct the cost of your own education (including certain related travel) related to your trade or business. You must be able to show the education maintains or improves skills required in your trade or business, or that it is required by law or regulations, for keeping your license to practice, status, or job. For example, an attorney can deduct the cost of attending Continuing Legal Education (CLE) classes that are required by the state bar association to maintain his or her license to practice law. Education expenses you incur to meet the minimum requirements of your present trade or business, or those that qualify you for a new trade or business, aren't deductible. This is true even if the education maintains or improves skills presently required in your business.

Franchise, trademark, trade name. If you buy a franchise, trademark, or trade name, you can deduct the amount you pay or incur as a business expense only if your payments are part of a series of payments that are:

1. Contingent on productivity, use, or disposition of the item;
2. Payable at least annually for the entire term of the transfer agreement; and
3. Substantially equal in amount (or payable under a fixed formula). When determining the term of the transfer agreement, include all renewal options and any other period for which you and the transferor reasonably expect the agreement to be renewed.

A franchise includes an agreement that gives one of the parties to the agreement the right to distribute, sell, or provide goods, services, or facilities within a specified area.

Impairment-related expenses. If you are disabled, you can deduct expenses necessary for you to be able to work (impairment-related expenses) as a business expense, rather than as a medical expense. You are disabled if you have either of the following.

- A physical or mental disability (for example, blindness or deafness) that functionally limits your being employed.
- A physical or mental impairment that substantially limits one or more of your major life activities. The expense qualifies as a business expense if all the following apply.
- Your work clearly requires the expense for you to satisfactorily perform that work.
- The goods or services purchased are clearly not needed or used, other than incidentally, in your personal activities.
- Their treatment isn't specifically provided for under other tax law provisions. Example. You are blind. You must use a reader to do your work, both at and away from your place of work. The reader's services are only for your work. You can deduct your expenses for the reader as a business expense. Internet-related expenses.

Generally, you can deduct Internet-related expenses including domain registration fees and webmaster consulting costs. If you are starting a business, you may have to amortize these expenses as start-up costs.

Interview expense allowances. Reimbursements you make to job candidates for transportation or other expenses related to interviews for possible employment aren't wages. You can deduct the reimbursements as a business expense. However, expenses for food, beverages, and entertainment are subject to the 50% limit discussed earlier under Meals and Entertainment.

Legal and professional fees. Fees charged by accountants and attorneys that are ordinary and necessary expenses directly related to operating your business are deductible as business expenses. However, usually legal fees you pay to acquire business assets aren't deductible. These costs are added to the basis of the property.

Fees that include payments for work of a personal nature (such as drafting a will, or damages arising from a personal injury) aren't allowed as a business deduction on Schedule C (Form 1040) or Schedule C-EZ (Form 1040). If the invoice includes both business and personal charges, figure the business portion as follows: multiply the total amount of the bill by a fraction, the numerator of which is the amount attributable to business matters, the denominator of which is the total amount paid. The result is the portion of the invoice attributable to business expenses.

The portion attributable to personal matters is the difference between the total amount and the business portion (figured above). Legal fees relating to doing or keeping your job, such as those you paid to defend yourself against criminal charges arising out of your trade or business, may be deductible on Schedule A (Form 1040), if you itemize deductions.

Certain payments made in sexual harassment or sexual abuse cases. For amounts paid or incurred after December 22, 2017, new section 162(q) provides that no deduction is allowed under section 162 for any settlement or payment related to sexual harassment or sexual abuse if it is subject to a nondisclosure agreement. In addition, attorney's fees related to such a settlement or payment are not allowed as a deduction.

Licenses and regulatory fees. Licenses and regulatory fees for your trade or business paid annually to state or local governments generally are deductible. Some licenses and fees may have to be amortized. See chapter 8 for more information. Lobbying expenses. Generally, lobbying expenses aren't deductible. Lobbying expenses include amounts paid or incurred for any of the following activities. • Influencing legislation.

- Participating in or intervening in any political campaign for, or against, any candidate for public office.
- Attempting to influence the general public, or segments of the public, about elections, legislative matters, or referendums.
- Communicating directly with covered executive branch officials (defined later) in any attempt to influence the official actions or positions of those officials.
- Researching, preparing, planning, or coordinating any of the preceding activities. Your expenses for influencing legislation and communicating directly with a covered executive branch official include a portion of your labor costs and general and administrative costs of your business.

You can't claim a charitable or business expense deduction for amounts paid to an organization if both of the following apply.

- The organization conducts lobbying activities on matters of direct financial interest to your business.

- A principal purpose of your contribution is to avoid the rules discussed earlier that prohibit a business deduction for lobbying expenses.

If a tax-exempt organization, other than a section 501(c)(3) organization, provides you with a notice on the part of dues that is allocable to nondeductible lobbying and political expenses, you can't deduct that part of the dues.

Covered executive branch official. For purposes of this discussion, a covered executive branch official is any of the following.

1. The President.
2. The Vice President.
3. Any officer or employee of the White House Office of the Executive Office of the President and the two most senior level officers of each of the other agencies in the Executive Office.
4. Any individual who:

a. Is serving in a position in Level I of the Executive Schedule under section 5312 of title 5, United States Code;
b. Has been designated by the President as having Cabinet-level status; or
c. Is an immediate deputy of an individual listed in item (a) or (b).

Exceptions to denial of deduction. The general denial of the deduction doesn't apply to the following.

- Any in-house expenses for influencing legislation and communicating directly with a covered executive branch official if those expenses for the tax year don't exceed $2,000 (excluding overhead expenses).
- Expenses incurred by taxpayers engaged in the trade or business of lobbying (professional lobbyists) on behalf of another person (but does apply to payments by the other person to the lobbyist for lobbying activities).

Moving machinery. Generally, the cost of moving machinery from one city to another is a deductible expense. So is the cost of moving machinery from one plant to another, or from one part of your plant to another. You can deduct the cost of installing the machinery in the new location. However, you must capitalize the costs of installing or moving newly purchased machinery.

Outplacement services. The costs of outplacement services you provide to your employees to help them find new employment, such as career counseling, résumé assistance, skills assessment, etc., are deductible. The costs of outplacement services may cover more than one deduction category. For example, deduct as a utility expense the cost of telephone calls made under this service and deduct as a rental expense the cost of renting machinery and equipment for this service.

Penalties and fines. Penalties paid for late performance or nonperformance of a contract are generally deductible. For instance, you own and operate a construction company. Under a contract, you are to finish construction of a building by a certain date. Due to construction delays, the building isn't completed and ready for occupancy on the date stipulated in the contract. You are now required to pay an additional amount for each day that completion is delayed beyond the completion date stipulated in the contract. These additional costs are deductible business expenses.

On the other hand, generally, no deduction is allowed for penalties and fines paid to a government or specified nongovernmental entity for the violation of any law except the following.

- Amounts that constitute restitution.
- Amounts paid to come into compliance with the law.
- Amounts paid or incurred as the result of certain court orders in which no government or specified nongovernmental agency is a party.
- Amounts paid or incurred for taxes due. On or after December 22, 2017, no deduction is allowed for the restitution amount or amount paid to come into compliance with the law unless the amounts are specifically identified in the settlement agreement or court order. Also, any amount paid or incurred as reimbursement to a government for the costs of any investigation or litigation are not eligible for the exceptions and are nondeductible. See section 162(f), as amended by P.L. 115-97, section 13306. Examples of nondeductible penalties and fines include the following.
- Amounts paid because of a conviction for a crime or after a plea of guilty or no contest in a criminal proceeding.
- Amounts paid as a penalty imposed by federal, state, or local law in a civil action, including certain additions to tax and additional amounts and assessable penalties imposed by the Internal Revenue Code
. • Amounts paid in settlement of actual or possible liability for a fine or penalty, whether civil or criminal.
- Amounts forfeited as collateral posted for a proceeding that could
result in a fine or penalty.

- Fines paid for violating city housing codes.
- Fines paid by truckers for violating state maximum highway weight laws.
- Fines paid for violating air quality laws.
- Civil penalties paid for violating federal laws regarding mining safety standards and discharges into navigable waters. A fine or penalty doesn't include any of the following.
- Legal fees and related expenses to defend yourself in a prosecution or civil action for a violation of the law imposing the fine or civil penalty.
- Court costs or stenographic and printing charges.
- Compensatory damages paid to a government.

Political contributions. Contributions or gifts paid to political parties or candidates aren't deductible. In addition, expenses paid or incurred to take part in any political campaign of a candidate for public office aren't deductible. Indirect political contributions.

You can't deduct indirect political contributions and costs of taking part in political activities as business expenses. Examples of nondeductible expenses include the following.

- Advertising in a convention program of a political party, or in any other publication if any of the proceeds from the publication are for, or intended for, the use of a political party or candidate.
- Admission to a dinner or program (including, but not limited to, galas, dances, film presentations, parties, and sporting events) if any of the proceeds from the function are for, or intended for, the use of a political party or candidate.
- Admission to an inaugural ball, gala, parade, concert, or similar event if identified with a political party or candidate.

Utilities. Business expenses for heat, lights, power, telephone service, and water and sewerage are deductible. However, any part due to personal use isn't deductible

Telephone. You can't deduct the cost of basic local telephone service (including any taxes) for the first telephone line you have in your home, even if you have an office in your home. However, charges for business long-distance phone calls on that line, as well as the cost of a second line into your home used exclusively for business, are deductible business expenses.

Transportation. You can deduct the cost of travel by airplane, train, bus, or car between your home and your business destination. Taxi, commuter bus, and limousine. You can deduct fares for these and other types of transportation between the airport or station and your hotel, or between the hotel and your work location away from home.

Baggage and shipping. You can deduct the cost of sending baggage and sample or display material between your regular and temporary work locations.

Car or truck. You can deduct the costs of operating and maintaining your vehicle when traveling away from home on business. You can deduct actual expenses or the standard mileage rate (discussed earlier under Car and Truck Expenses), as well as business-related tolls and parking. If you rent a car while away from home on business, you can deduct only the business-use portion of the expenses.

Meals and lodging. You can deduct the cost of meals and lodging if your business trip is overnight or long enough that you need to stop for sleep or rest to properly perform your duties. You can use actual expenses or standard meal allowance to calculate your deduction. In most cases, you can deduct only 50% of your meal expenses.

Cleaning. You can deduct the costs of dry cleaning and laundry while on your business trip. Telephone. You can deduct the cost of business calls while on your business trip, including business communication by fax machine or other communication devices.

Tips. You can deduct the tips you pay for any expense in this list.

Reimbursing your employees for expenses. You generally can deduct the amount you reimburse your employees for travel and meal expenses. The reimbursement you deduct and the way you deduct it depend in part on whether you reimburse the expenses under an accountable plan or a nonaccountable plan.

Business Use of Your Home

To deduct expenses related to the part of your home used for business, you must meet specific requirements. Even then, your deduction may be limited. To qualify to claim expenses for business use of your home, you must meet the following tests.

    1. Your use of the business part of your home must be:

Exclusive (however, see Exceptions to exclusive use, later);

Regular;

For your business; and

    2. The business part of your home must be one of the following:

Your principal place of business (defined later);

A place where you meet or deal with patients, clients, or customers in the normal course of your business; or

A separate structure (not attached to your home) It includes the entire city or general area in which your business is located.

The following is a brief discussion of the expenses you can deduct.

The business use of your home under the principal place of business test, your home must be your principal place of business for that business. To determine your principal place of business, you must consider all the facts and circumstances. Your home office will qualify as your principal place of business for deducting expenses for its use if you meet the following requirements.

- You use it exclusively and regularly for administrative or management activities of your business.
- You have no other fixed location where you conduct substantial administrative or management activities of your business. Alternatively, if you use your home exclusively and regularly for your business, but your home office does not qualify as your principal place of business based on the previous rules, you determine your principal place of business based on the following factors.
- The relative importance of the activities performed at each location.
- If the relative importance factor does not determine your principal place of business, you also can consider the time spent at each location.

Exceptions to Exclusive Use

You do not have to meet the exclusive use test to the extent you se part of your home in either of the following ways.
For the storage of inventory or product samples. As
a daycare facility.

If, after considering your business locations, your home cannot be identified as your principal place of business, you cannot deduct home office expenses. However, for other ways to qualify to deduct home office expenses, see IRS Pub. 587.

Deduction Limit

If your gross income from the business use of your home equals or exceeds your total business expenses (including depreciation), you can deduct all your business expenses related to the use of your home. If your gross income from the business use is less than your total business expenses, your deduction for certain expenses for the business use of your home is limited.

Your deduction of otherwise nondeductible expenses, such as insurance, utilities, and depreciation (with depreciation taken last), allocable to the business is limited to the gross income from the business use of your home minus the sum of the following.

1. The business part of expenses you could deduct even if you did not use your home for business (such as mortgage interest, real estate taxes, and casualty and theft losses that are allowable as itemized deductions on Schedule A (Form 1040)).

2. The business expenses that relate to the business activity in the home (for example, business phone, supplies, and depreciation on equipment), but not to the use of the home itself. Do not include in (2) above your deduction for one-half of your self-employment tax.

Use Form 8829, **Expenses for Business Use of Your Home,** to figure your deduction.

Simplified Method.

The IRS provides a simplified method to determine your expenses for business use of your home. The simplified method is an alternative to calculating and substantiating actual expenses. In most cases, you will figure your deduction by multiplying $5 by the area of your home used for a qualified business use. The area you use to figure your deduction is limited to 300 square feet. For more information, see the Instructions for Schedule C.

De Minimis Safe Harbor for Tangible Property

Generally, you must capitalize costs to acquire or produce real or tangible personal property used in your trade or business, such as buildings, equipment, or furniture. However, if you elect to use the de minimis safe harbor for tangible property, you may deduct de minimis amounts paid to acquire or produce certain tangible property if these amounts are deducted by you for financial accounting purposes or in keeping your books and records. If you have an applicable financial statement, you may use this safe harbor to deduct amounts paid for tangible property up to $5,000 per item or invoice. If you do not have an applicable financial statement, you may use the de minimis safe harbor to deduct amounts paid for tangible property up to $2,500 per item or invoice. Amounts qualifying under this de minimis safe harbor should be included as other expenses in Part V of Schedule C.

Other Expenses You Can Deduct

You also may be able to deduct the following expenses.
- Advertising.
- Bank fees.
- Donations to business organizations.
- Education expenses.
- Impairment-related expenses.
- Interview expense allowances.
- Licenses and regulatory fees.
- Moving machinery.

- Outplacement services.
- Penalties and fines you pay for late performance or nonperformance of a contract.
- Repairs and maintenance to real or tangible personal property.
- Repayments of income.
- Subscriptions to trade or professional publications.
- Supplies and materials.
- Utilities.

Qualified Business Income Deduction

The qualified business income deduction known as QBI is a deduction from your "qualified business income". This deduction allows you to deduct up to 20 percent of the qualified business income (QBI) of the business. This deduction is available for tax years beginning after December 31, 2017. It can be claimed starting with the 2018 return.

This qualified business income deduction is a complicated formula. It involves two components.

QBI Component This component of the deduction equals 20 percent of QBI from a domestic business operated as a sole proprietorship or through a partnership, S corporation, trust or estate. There are limitations regarding certain types of businesses, W-2 wages paid by the qualified trade or business and the adjusted basis immediately after acquisition of qualified property held by the trade or business.

These limitations do not apply to taxpayers with taxable income at or below a certain threshold. For 2018, the threshold amount is $315,000 for a married couple filing a joint return, and $157,500 for all other taxpayers.

REIT/PTP Component This component of the deduction equals 20 percent of qualified REIT dividends and qualified PTP income. This component is not limited by W-2 wages or UBIA of qualified property. Depending on the taxpayer's taxable income, the amount of PTP income that qualifies may be limited if the PTP is engaged in a specified service trade or business.

The deduction is limited to the lesser of the QBI component plus the REIT/PTP component or 20 percent of the taxable income minus net capital gain. The deduction is available regardless of whether an individual itemizes their deductions on Schedule A or takes the standard deduction.

Qualified Trade or Business

A qualified trade or business is any section 162 trade or business, with three exceptions:
A trade or business conducted by a C corporation.

For taxpayers with taxable income that exceeds the threshold amount, specified services trades or business (SSTBs). An SSTB is a trade or business involving the performance of services in the fields of health, law, accounting, actuarial science, performing arts, consulting, athletics, financial services, investing and investment management, trading, dealing in certain assets or any trade or business principal asset is the reputation or skill of one or more of its employees or owners.

The principal asset of a trade or business is the reputation or skill of its employees or owners if the trade or business consists of the receipt of income from endorsing products or services, the use of an individual's image, likeness, voice or other symbols associated with the individual's identity, or appearance at events or on radio, television and other media outlets.

For 2018, the threshold amount is $315,000 for a married couple filing a joint return, and $157,500 for all other taxpayers. The SSTB limitations don't apply for taxpayers with taxable income at or below the threshold amount. Limitations are phased in for joint filers with taxable income between
$315,000 and $415,000, and all other taxpayers with taxable income between $157,500 and $207,500. For later years, the threshold amounts, and phase-in range will be adjusted for inflation.

Qualified Business Income

QBI is the net amount of qualified items of income, gain, deduction and loss from any qualified trade or business, including income from partnerships, S corporations, sole proprietorships, and certain trusts. These includable items must be effectively connected with the conduct of a trade or business within the United States. Count only items in taxable income. Generally, in computing QBI, account for any deduction attributable to the trade or business. This includes, but is not limited to, the deductible part of self-employment tax, self-employed health insurance, and deductions for contributions to qualified retirement plans (such as SEP, SIMPLE and qualified plan deductions).

QBI doesn't include any of the following.

Items not properly includible in income, such as losses or deductions disallowed under the basis, at-risk, passive loss or excess business loss rules.

Investment items such as capital gains or losses, or dividends.

Interest income not properly allocable to a trade or business.

Wage income.

Income not effectively connected with the conduct of business within the U.S.

Commodities transactions or foreign currency gains or losses.

Income, loss, or deductions from notional principal contracts.

Annuities (unless received in connection with the trade or business).

Amounts received as reasonable compensation from an S corporation.

Amounts received as guaranteed payments from a partnership.

Payments received by a partner for services other than in a capacity as a partner.

Qualified REIT dividends. Qualified PTP income.

Rental Real Estate Enterprise Safe Harbor

Solely for the purposes of 199A, a safe harbor is available to individuals and owners of passthrough entities. Under the safe harbor a rental real estate enterprise will be treated as a trade or business for purposes of the QBI deduction.

Taxpayers may still treat rental real estate that doesn't meet the requirements of the safe harbor as a trade or business for purposes of the QBI deduction if it is a section 162 trade or business.

Don't worry if this seems confusing. This deduction will automatically compute when you file your taxes using tax software. There are several good tax software packages out there or you can contact an enrolled agent, CPA, or tax attorney to file your return for you.

Expenses You Cannot Deduct

You usually cannot deduct the following as business expenses.
- Bribes and kickbacks.
- Charitable contributions.
- Demolition expenses or losses.
- Dues to business, social, athletic, luncheon, sporting, airline, and hotel clubs.
- Entertainment expenses.
- Improvements to real or tangible personal property. Improvements are amounts paid for betterments to your property, restorations of your property, or work that adapts your property to a new or different use.
- Lobbying expenses.
- Penalties and fines you pay to a governmental agency or instrumentality because you broke the law.
- Personal, living, and family expenses.
- Political contributions
- Settlements or payments related to sexual harassment or sexual abuse if such settlement or payment is subject to a nondisclosure agreement. You also cannot deduct attorney fees related to such settlement or payment.

CHAPTER SEVEN

GROSS PROFIT AND NET PROFIT

Figuring Gross Profit Introduction

After you have figured the gross receipts from your business and the cost of goods sold, you are ready to figure your gross profit. You must determine gross profit before you can deduct any business expenses. If you are filing Schedule C-EZ, your gross profit is your gross receipts plus certain other amounts, explained later under Additions to Gross Profit.

Businesses That Sell Products

If you are filing Schedule C, figure your gross profit by first figuring your net receipts. Figure net receipts (line 3) on Schedule C by subtracting any returns and allowances (line 2) from gross receipts (line 1). Returns and allowances include cash or credit refunds you make to customers, rebates, and other allowances off the actual sales price. Next, subtract the cost of goods sold (line 4) from net receipts (line 3). The result is the gross profit from your business.

Businesses That Sell Services

You do not have to figure the cost of goods sold if the sale of merchandise is not an income-producing factor for your business. Your gross profit is the same as your net receipts (gross receipts minus any refunds, rebates, or other allowances). Most professions and businesses that sell services rather than products can figure gross profit directly from net receipts.

Illustration. The gross profit section of the income statement of a retail business shows how gross profit is figured.

Income Statement Year Ended December 31, 2018

Gross receipts $400,000
Minus:
Returns and allowances 14,940
Equals:
Net receipts $385,060
Minus:
Cost of goods sold 288,140
Equals:
Gross profit $96,920

The cost of goods sold for this business is figured as follows.
Inventory at beginning of year $37,845
Purchases $285,900
Minus:
Items withdrawn for personal use ... 2,650
  Plus:
Net Purchases.......................................283,250
Equals:
Goods available for sale $321,095
Minus: Inventory at end of year 32,955
Equals:
Cost of goods sold $288,140

Items to Check

Gross receipts. At the end of each business day, make sure your records balance with your actual cash and credit receipts for the day. You may find it helpful to use cash registers to keep track of receipts. You also should use a proper invoicing system and keep a separate bank account for your business.

Sales tax collected. Check to make sure your records show the correct sales tax collected. If you collect state and local sales taxes imposed on you as the seller of goods or services from the buyer, you must include the amount collected in gross receipts. If you are required to collect state and local taxes imposed on the buyer and turn them over to state or local governments, you generally do not include these amounts in income.

Inventory at beginning of year. Compare this figure with last year's ending inventory. The two amounts should usually be the same.

Purchases. If you take any inventory items for your personal use (use them yourself, provide them to your family, or give them as personal gifts, etc.) be sure to remove them from the cost of goods sold.

Inventory at end of year. Check to make sure your procedures for taking inventory are adequate. These procedures should ensure all items have been included in inventory and proper pricing techniques have been used. Use inventory forms and adding machine tapes as the only evidence for your inventory. Inventory forms are available at office supply stores. These forms have columns for recording the description, quantity, unit price, and value of each inventory item. Each page has space to record who made the physical count, who priced the items, who made the extensions, and who proofread the calculations. These forms will help satisfy you that the total inventory is accurate. They also will provide you with a permanent record to support its validity.

Testing Gross Profit Accuracy If you are in a retail or wholesale business, you can check the accuracy of your gross profit figure. First, divide gross profit by net receipts. The resulting percentage measures the average spread between the merchandise cost of goods sold and the selling price. Next, compare this percentage to your markup policy. Little or no difference between these two percentages shows that your gross profit figure is accurate.

A large difference between these percentages may show that you did not accurately figure sales, purchases, inventory, or other items of cost. You should determine the reason for the difference. **Example.** Joe Able operates a retail business. On the average, he marks up his merchandise so that he will realize a gross profit of 331/3% on its sales. The net receipts (gross receipts minus returns and allowances) shown on his income statement is $300,000. His cost of goods sold is $200,000. This results in a gross profit of $100,000 ($300,000 − $200,000). To test the accuracy of this year's results, Joe divides gross profit ($100,000) by net receipts ($300,000). The resulting 331/3% confirms his markup percentage of 331/3%.

Additions to Gross Profit

If your business has income from a source other than its regular business operations, enter the income on line 6 of Schedule C and add it to gross profit. The result is gross business income. If you use Schedule C-EZ, include the income on line 1 of the schedule. Some examples include income from an interest-bearing checking account, income from scrap sales, income from certain fuel tax credits and refunds, and amounts recovered from bad debts.

NET PROFIT

After figuring your business income and expenses, you are ready to figure the net profit or net loss from your business. You do this by subtracting business expenses from business income. If your expenses are less than your income, the difference is net profit and becomes part of your income on line 12 of Schedule 1 (Form 1040). If your expenses are more than your income, the difference is a net loss. You usually can deduct it from gross income on line 12 of Schedule 1 (Form 1040).

But in some situations, your loss is limited.

This chapter briefly explains three of those situations. Other situations that may limit your loss are explained in the instructions for Schedule C, line G and line 32. If you have more than one business, you must figure your net profit or loss for each business on a separate Schedule C. Excess Business Loss Limitation Your loss from a trade or business may be limited. Use Form 461 to determine the amount of your excess business loss, if any. Your excess business loss will be included as income on line 21 of Schedule 1 (Form 1040) and treated as a net operating loss that you must carry forward and deduct in a subsequent year. Your excess business loss will not be reflected on your Schedule C or C-EZ.

Net Operating Losses (NOLs) If your deductions for the year are more than your income for the year (line 10 of your Form 1040 is not more than zero), you may have a net operating loss (NOL). You can use an NOL by deducting it from your income in another year or years.

Examples of typical losses that may produce an NOL include, but are not limited to, losses incurred from the following.

- Your trade or business.
- A casualty or theft resulting from a federally declared disaster.
- Moving expenses.
- Rental property. A loss from operating a business is the most common reason for an NOL.

Not-for-Profit Activities If you do not carry on your business to make a profit, there is a limit on the deductions you can take. You cannot use a loss from the activity to offset other income. Activities you do as a hobby, or mainly for sport or recreation, come under this limit.

CHAPTER EIGHT

FILING AND PAYING TAXES

This chapter explains the business taxes you may have to pay and the forms you may have to file. It also discusses taxpayer identification numbers.

Identification Numbers

This section explains three types of taxpayer identification numbers, who needs them, when to use them, and how to get them.

Social security number (SSN). Generally, use your SSN as your taxpayer identification number. You must put this number on each of your individual income tax forms, such as Form 1040 and its schedules. To apply for an SSN, use Form SS-5, Application for a Social Security Card. This form is available at Social Security Administration (SSA) offices or by calling 1-800-772-1213. It is also available from the SSA website at SSA.gov.

Individual taxpayer identification number (ITIN). The IRS will issue an ITIN if you are a nonresident or resident alien and you do not have and are not eligible to get an SSN. The ITIN will expire for any taxpayer who does not file a federal income tax return (or who is not included as a dependent on the return of another taxpayer) for three consecutive years. In general, if you need to obtain an ITIN, you must attach Form W-7, Application for IRS Individual Taxpayer Identification Number, with your signed, original, completed tax return and any other required documentation and mail them to the address in the Instructions for Form W-7. Exceptions are covered in the instructions.

The application is also available in Spanish. The form is available at IRS.gov/ Order Forms. An ITIN is for tax use only. It does not entitle the holder to social security benefits or change the holder's employment or immigration status.

Employer identification number (EIN). You also must have an EIN to use as a taxpayer identification number if you do either of the following . • Pay wages to one or more employees.

• File pension or excise tax returns. If you must have an EIN, include it along with your SSN on your Schedule C or C-EZ as instructed.

How to Get an EIN:

Online by clicking on the Employer ID Numbers (EINs) link at IRS.gov/Businesses/Small if the principal business location is in the United States or U.S. territories. The EIN is issued immediately once the application information is validated.

By telephone at 267-941-1099 (not a toll-free number) only if the principal business is located outside the United States or U.S. Territories.

By mailing or faxing Form SS-4, Application for Employer Identification Number. New EIN. You may need to get a new EIN if either the form or the ownership of your business changes In operating your business, you will probably make certain payments you must report on information returns.

You must give the recipient of these payments (the payee) a statement showing the total amount paid during the year. You must include the payee's identification number and your identification number on the returns and statements.

Employees

If you have employees, you must get an SSN from each of them. Record the name and SSN of each employee exactly as they are shown on the employee's social security card. If the employee's name is not correct as shown on the card, the employee should request a new card from the SSA. This may occur if the employee's name was changed due to marriage or divorce.

Form W-4, is completed by each employee so the correct federal income tax can be withheld from their pay. If your employee does not have an SSN, he or she should file Form SS-5 with the SSA.

Other payee. If you make payments to someone who is not your employee and you must report the payments on an information return, get that person's SSN. If you must report payments to an organization, such as a corporation or partnership, you must get its EIN.

To get the payee's SSN or EIN, use Form W-9, Request for Taxpayer Identification Number and Certification. A payee who does not provide you with an identification number may be subject to backup withholding. For information on backup withholding, see the Instructions for the Requester of Form W-9 and the General Instructions for Certain Information Returns.

If you have employees, you will need to file quarterly 940 tax forms due April 30th, July 31st, October 31st and January 31st. You, also, must file the annual 941 tax from. Check IRS pub 15 Employer's Tax Guide, for more information.

You are required to make federal tax deposits for employee taxes withheld and any employer match for social security, etc. You may make your payment with a timely filed form 941 or form 944 in most instances.

However, some employers are required to make monthly tax deposits if their employee taxes exceed $50,000 for the four previous quarters. There is, also, a $100,000 next day deposit rule. Some employers use a payroll tax service if they have employees. This way your quarterly and annual forms will be prepared and presented to you to sign and enclose payroll taxes due.

Income Tax

This part explains whether you must file an income tax return and when you file it. It also explains how you pay the tax.

Do I Have to File an Income Tax Return? You must file an income tax return for 2018 if your net earnings from self-employment were $400 or more. If your net earnings from self-employment were less than $400, you still must file an income tax return if you meet any other filing requirement listed in the Instructions for Form 1040.

How Do I File? File your income tax return on Form 1040 and attach Schedule C or Schedule C-EZ. Enter the net profit or loss from Schedule C or Schedule C-EZ on Schedule 1 (Form 1040). Use Schedule C to figure your net profit or loss from your business. If you operated more than one business as a sole proprietorship, you must attach a separate Schedule C for each business.

You can use the simpler Schedule C-EZ if you operated only one business as a sole proprietorship, you did not have a net loss, and you meet the other requirements listed in Part I of the schedule.

IRS e-file (Electronic Filing)

You may be able to file your tax returns electronically using an IRS e-file option. IRS e-file uses automation to replace most of the manual steps needed to process paper returns. As a result, the processing of e-file returns is faster and more accurate than the processing of paper returns. As with a paper return, you are responsible for making sure your return contains accurate information and is filed on time. Using e-file does not affect your chances of an IRS examination of your return. You can file most commonly used business forms using IRS e-file.

Paperless filing is easier than you think and it's available to most taxpayers who file electronically including those first-time filers who were 16 or older at the end of 2019. If you file electronically using tax preparation software or a tax professional, you will sign your return using the Self-Select PIN (personal identification number) Method for e-file.

If you are married filing jointly, you and your spouse will each need to create a PIN and enter these PINs as your electronic signatures. To create a PIN, you must know your adjusted gross income (AGI) from your originally filed 2017 income tax return (not from an amended return, Form 1040X, or any math error notice from the IRS). You also will need to provide your date of birth (DOB). Make sure your DOB is accurate and matches the information on record with the Social Security Administration before you e-file. To do this, check your annual Social Security Statement.

With a Self-Select PIN, there is nothing to sign and nothing to mail—not even your Forms W-2.

State Returns

In most states, you can file an electronic state return simultaneously with your federal return. For more information, check with your local IRS office, state tax agency, tax professional, or IRS.gov.

Refunds

You can have your refund check mailed to you, or you can have your refund deposited directly to your checking or savings account. With e-file, your refund will be issued in half the time as when filing on paper. Most refunds are issued in less than 21 days.

Offset Against Debts

As with a paper return, you may not get all of your refund if you owe certain past-due amounts, such as federal tax, state tax, a student loan, or child support. You will be notified if the refund you claimed has been offset against your debts.

Refund Inquiries

You can check the status of your refund if it has been at least 24 hours (4 weeks if you mailed a paper return) from the date you filed your return. Be sure to have a copy of your tax return available because you will need to know the filing status, the first social security number shown on the return, and the exact whole-dollar amount of the refund. To check on your refund, do one of the following.

- Go to IRS.gov/Refunds.

- Download the free IRS2Go app to your smart phone and use it to check your refund status.
- Call 800-829-1954 for automated refund information and follow the recorded instructions.

When Is My Tax Return Due?

Form 1040 for calendar year 2018 is due by April 15, 2019. If you use a fiscal year, your return is due by the 15th day of the 4th month after the end of your fiscal year. If you file late, you may have to pay penalties and interest.

If You Cannot File Your Return on Time

Use form 4868, **Application for Automatic Extension of Time to File U.S. Individual Income Tax Return,** to request an automatic 6-month extension. For calendar year taxpayers, this will extend the tax filing due date until October 15th. Filing an extension does not extend the time that your tax payments are due.

CHAPTER NINE

YOUR RIGHTS AS A TAXPAYER

The first part of this chapter explains some of your most important rights as a taxpayer. The second part explains the examination, appeal, collection, and refund processes.
The following is reprinted verbatim from the IRS.

Taxpayer Bill of Rights

All taxpayers have fundamental rights they should be aware of when dealing with the IRS. The Taxpayer Bill of Rights, which the IRS adopted in June of 2014, takes existing rights in the tax code and groups them into the following 10 broad categories, making them easier to understand.
Explore your rights and our obligations to protect them.
The right to be informed. Taxpayers have the right to know what they need to do to comply with the tax laws

. They are entitled to clear explanations of the laws and IRS procedures in all tax forms, instructions, publications, notices, and correspondence.

They have the right to be informed of IRS decisions about their tax accounts and to receive clear explanations of the outcomes.

The right to quality service. Taxpayers have the right to receive prompt, courteous, and professional assistance in their dealings with the IRS, to be spoken to in a way they can easily understand, to receive clear and easily understandable communications from the IRS, and to speak to a supervisor about inadequate service.

The right to pay no more than the correct amount of tax. Taxpayers have the right to pay only the amount of tax legally due, including interest and penalties, and to have the IRS apply all tax payments properly.

The right to challenge the IRS's position and be heard. Taxpayers have the right to raise objections and provide additional documentation in response to formal IRS actions or proposed actions, to expect that the IRS will consider their timely objections and documentation promptly and fairly, and to receive a response if the IRS does not agree with their position.

The right to appeal an IRS decision in an independent forum. Taxpayers are entitled to a fair and impartial administrative appeal of most IRS decisions, including many penalties, and have the right to receive a written response regarding the Office of Appeals' decision.

Taxpayers generally have the right to take their cases to court. The right to finality. Taxpayers have the right to know the maximum amount of time they have to challenge the IRS's position as well as the maximum amount of time the IRS has to audit a particular tax year or collect a tax debt.

Taxpayers have the right to know when the IRS has finished an audit. The right to privacy. Taxpayers have the right to expect that any IRS inquiry, examination, or enforcement action will comply with the law and be no more intrusive than necessary, and will respect all due process rights, including search and seizure protections, and will provide, where applicable, a collection due process hearing.

The right to confidentiality. Taxpayers have the right to expect that any information they provide to the IRS will not be disclosed unless authorized by the taxpayer or by law.

Taxpayers have the right to expect appropriate action will be taken against employees, return preparers, and others who wrongfully use or disclose taxpayer return information.

The right to retain representation. Taxpayers have the right to retain an authorized representative of their choice to represent them in their dealings with the IRS. Taxpayers have the right to seek assistance from a Low-Income Taxpayer Clinic if they cannot afford representation.

The right to a fair and just tax system. Taxpayers have the right to expect the tax system to consider facts and circumstances that might affect their underlying liabilities, ability to pay, or ability to provide information timely. Taxpayers have the right to receive assistance from the Taxpayer Advocate Service if they are experiencing financial difficulty or if the IRS has not resolved their tax issues properly and timely through its normal channels.

Examinations, Appeals, Collections, and Refunds
Examinations (audits)

We accept most taxpayers' returns as filed. If we inquire about your return or select it for examination, it does not suggest that you are dishonest. The inquiry or examination may or may not result in more tax. We may close your case without change; or, you may receive a refund. The process of selecting a return for examination usually begins in one of two ways. First, we use computer programs to identify returns that may have incorrect amounts. These programs may be based on information returns, such as Forms 1099 and W-2, on studies of past examinations, or on certain issues identified by compliance projects. Second, we use information from outside sources that indicates that a return may have incorrect amounts. These sources may include newspapers, public records, and individuals. If we determine that the information is accurate and reliable, we may use it to select a return for examination

Publication 556, Examination of Returns, Appeal Rights, and Claims for Refund explains the rules and procedures that we follow in examinations. The following sections give an overview of how we conduct examinations.

By mail. We handle many examinations and inquiries by mail. We will send you a letter with either a request for more information or a reason why we believe a change to your return may be needed. You can respond by mail or you can request a personal interview with an examiner. If you mail us the requested information or provide an explanation, we may or may not agree with you, and we will explain the reasons for any changes. Please do not hesitate to write to us about anything you do not understand.

By interview. If we notify you that we will conduct your examination through a personal interview, or you request such an interview, you have the right to ask that the examination take place at a reasonable time and place that is convenient for both you and the IRS. If our examiner proposes any changes to your return, he or she will explain the reasons for the changes. If you do not agree with these changes, you can meet with the examiner's supervisor.

Repeat examinations. If we examined your return for the same items in either of the 2 previous years and proposed no change to your tax liability, please contact us as soon as possible so we can see if we should discontinue the examination.

Appeals

If you do not agree with the examiner's proposed changes, you can appeal them to the Appeals Office of the IRS. Most differences can be settled without expensive and time-consuming court trials. Your appeal rights are explained in detail in both Publication 5, Your Appeal Rights and How To Prepare a Protest If You Don't Agree, and Publication 556, Examination of Returns, Appeal Rights, and Claims for Refund. If you do not wish to use the Appeals Office or disagree with its findings, you may be able to take your case to the U.S. Tax Court, U.S. Court of Federal Claims, or the U.S. District Court where you live. If you take your case to court, the IRS will have the burden of proving certain facts if you kept adequate records to show your tax liability, cooperated with the IRS, and meet certain other conditions. If the court agrees with you on most issues in your case and finds that our position was largely unjustified, you may be able to recover some of your administrative and litigation costs. You will not be eligible to recover these costs unless you tried to resolve your case administratively, including going through the appeals system, and you gave us the information necessary to resolve the case.

Collections

Publication 594, The IRS Collection Process, explains your rights and responsibilities regarding payment of federal taxes. It describes:

- **What to do when you owe taxes**. It describes what to do if you get a tax bill and what to do if you think your bill is wrong. It also covers making installment payments, delaying collection action, and submitting an offer in compromise.
- **IRS collection actions**. It covers liens, releasing a lien, levies, releasing a levy, seizures and sales, and release of property.
- **IRS certification to the State Department of a seriously delinquent tax debt**, which will generally result in denial of a passport application and may lead to revocation of a passport. Your collection appeal rights are explained in detail in Publication 1660, Collection Appeal Rights.

Innocent spouse relief. Generally, both you and your spouse are responsible, jointly and individually, for paying the full amount of any tax, interest, or penalties due on your joint return. To seek relief from any liability related to your spouse (or former spouse), you must file a claim on Form 8857, Request for Innocent Spouse Relief cases, Form 8857 may need to be filed within 2 years of the date on which the IRS first attempted to collect the tax from you. Do not file Form 8857 with your Form 1040. For more information, see Publication 971, Innocent Spouse Relief, and Form 8857 or you can call the Innocent Spouse office toll free at 855-851-2009.

Potential Third-Party Contacts

Generally, the IRS will deal directly with you or your duly authorized representative. However, we sometimes talk with other persons if we need information that you have been unable to provide, or to verify information we have received. If we do contact other persons, such as a neighbor, bank, employer, or employees, we will generally need to tell them limited information, such as your name. The law prohibits us from disclosing any more information than is necessary to obtain or verify the information we are seeking. Our need to contact other persons may continue as long as there is activity in your case. If we do contact other persons, you have a right to request a list of those contacted. Your request can be made by telephone, in writing, or during a personal interview.

Refunds

You can file a claim for refund if you think you paid too much tax. You generally must file the claim within 3 years from the date you filed your original return or 2 years from the date you paid the tax, whichever is later. The law generally provides for interest on your refund if it is not paid within 45 days of the date you filed your return or claim for refund. Publication 556, Examination of Returns, Appeal Rights, and Claims for Refund has more information on refunds. If you were due a refund but you did not file a return, you must file within 3 years from the date the return was due (including extensions) to get that refund.

CHAPTER TEN

COMMON TAX MISTAKES to AVOID

Not keeping good records

Over reporting Income

Under reporting income

Forgetting carryovers

Misclassifying employees

Not separating expenses

Not identifying all expenses deductible

Filing and paying estimated taxes late

Getting behind on tax deposits and estimated payments

Choosing the wrong form of business

And the number one mistake many people make is failing to respond when IRS contacts them. When you receive a letter from IRS, read it and respond. However, if you don't understand it or it frightens you, contact your accountant.

Never ignore IRS when they notify you because the clock is clicking. Interest and penalties continue to pile up and the amount you owe will continue to multiply while you do nothing.

CHAPTER ELEVEN

HOW TO GET MORE INFORMATION

You can contact Charlotte Allen at smallbizcure@gmail.com.

My website: https://smallbusinesscure.com

Follow Charlotte Allen on twitter: FromMyViewPoint

Federal Tax Information: www.irs.gov

Questions regarding business formation: www.sba.gov

STATE INFORMATION

Each state has its own rules and regulations. A discussion of taxes for each of the states is beyond the scope of this book. State taxation will vary from state to state. States follow the basics of Federal taxation for income but there are modifications for certain expenses such as depreciation. For example, Federal taxation allows for various methods for depreciating the assets of a business whereas states might only use straight line depreciation. There are other adjustments depending on the state.

I have listed the websites of each state so you can obtain more information. Below is the website address for each state.

Alabama	Revenue.alabama.gov/audience/businesses
Alaska	Tax.state.ak.us
Arizona	Azdor.gov
Arkansas	Portal.arkansas.gov/pages/taxes-in-arkansas
California	Ftb.ca.gov
Colorado	Colorado.gov/ftb.ca.gov
Connecticut	Portal.ct.gov/drs
Delaware	Revenue.delaware.gov
District of Columbia	Otr.cfo.dc.gov/service/business-taxpayers
Florida	Floridarevenue.com/pages/info-business.aspx
Georgia	Dor.georgia.gov
Hawaii	Tax.hawaii.gov
Idaho	Tax.idaho.gov
Illinois	www2.illinois.gov/rev/Business/pages/default.aspx
Indiana	In.gov/dor/
Iowa	Tax.iowa.gov
Kansas	Ksrevenue.org
Kentucky	Revenue.Ky.gov/pages/index.aspx

Louisiana	Revenue.louisiana.gov/Businesses
Maine	Maine.gov/Revenue/
Maryland	Taxes.Marylandtaxes.gov/business-taxes/
Massachusetts	Mass.gov/orgs/Massachusetts-department-of Revenue
Michigan	Michigan.gov/taxes/0.4676.7-238-43519---,00.html
Minnesota	Revenue.state.mn.us/businesses
Mississippi	Dor.ms.gov/pages/default.aspx
Missouri	Dor.mo.gov/business/
Montana	Mtrevenue.gov
Nebraska	Revenue.nebraska.gov/busi.nc.html
Nevada	Tax.nv.gov
New Hampshire	Revenue.nh.gov
New Jersey	State.nj.us/treasury/taxation
New Mexico	Tax.newmexico.gov/default.aspx
New York	Tax.ny.gov
North Carolina	Ncdor.gov
North Dakota	Nd.gov/tax/
Ohio	Tax.ohio.gov
Oklahoma	Ok.gov/tax/
Oregon	Oregon.gov/dor/pages/index.aspx
Pennsylvania	Revenue.pa.gov/pages/default.aspx
Rhode Island	Tax.ri.gov
South Carolina	Dor.sc.gov
South Dakota	Dor.sd.gov
Tennessee	tn.gov/revenue/
Texas	Comptroller.texas.gov/business
Utah	Tax.utah.gov/business

Vermont	Tax.vermont.gov/
Virginia	Tax.virginia.gov
Washington	Dor.wa.gov
West Virginia	Tax.wv.gov/pages/default.aspx
Wisconsin	Revenue.wi.gov/pages/businesses/home.aspx
Wyoming	Revenue.wyo.gov

Disclaimer: Federal tax laws are constantly changing. The information in this book is current as of the filing date. Depending on your individual situation you may need more detailed information. If so, contact one of the sources above or ask your accountant.

www.ingramcontent.com/pod-product-compliance
Lightning Source LLC
Chambersburg PA
CBHW020543220526
45463CB00006B/2178